Magic Salsa

125 Naturally Low-Fat Bold and Brassy Sauces to Add Flavor to Any Meal

David Woods

CHRONIMED PUBLISHING

Magic Salsa: 125 Naturally Low-Fat Bold and
Brassy Sauces to Add Flavor to Any Meal © 1998
by David Woods

Library of Congress Cataloging-in-Publication Data
Woods, David
Magic salsa / by David Woods

       p.   cm.

Includes index.

ISBN 1-56561-147-0; $14.95

Edited by: Jolene Steffer
Cover Design: Garborg Design Works
Text Design & Production: David Enyeart
Art/Production Manager: Claire Lewis
Nutrition Information: Sandra Nissenberg, RD

Printed in the United States

Published by
Chronimed Publishing
P.O. Box 59032
Minneapolis, MN 55459-0032

10   9   8   7   6   5   4   3   2   1

Introduction

Salsa! In Spanish salsa means sauce. That well known sauce of Mexico and other Latin American countries has topped ketchup in dollar volume in the United States. Some feel that it is just for dipping with tortilla chips or topping over nachos and green salads. Typically a tomato based combo, it is more interesting to make out of a wide variety of ingredients. Salsa can be made from chopped fruits or vegetables, combined into a fresh or cooked sauce. The common denominator in salsas is chilies, even in the fruit salsas, but nothing is out of bounds. With their vibrant mix of colors, flavors, and textures, from hot and spicy to sweet and tangy, salsa is one of the best and easiest ways to complement any meal from appetizer to dessert.

In this book, three distinct styles of salsa are presented: uncooked, cooked, and a combination of cooked and uncooked ingredients. They were inspired by Latin American and Mexican friends and neighbors who shared their ideas and refined the recipes in our kitchen for maximum flavor and appearance. Each recipe carries at least one serving suggestion, but remember: There are no rules! Feel free to experiment by adjusting ingredients to taste and pairing salsas with your own favorite meals.

Uncooked salsas are deceptively simple in appearance and yet must balance opposing textures, flavors, and spices in an attractive and tasty manner. They are only as flavorful as their ingredients, so it is important to utilize only the highest quality fruits and vegetables at the peak of their individual seasons. Recipes range from brassy and bold to sweet and inviting. Uncooked salsas are never shy or retiring, and so are best served with simply prepared fish, meat, poultry, or steamed vegetables, or tossed with cold pasta. Most chip dip salsas are also raw. An assortment of sharp knives, a potato peeler, and a citrus zester are important tools in making uncooked salsas.

Cooked salsas are not as fussy as continental sauces but possess a similarly smooth, velvety consistency and underlying richness. Dairy products are rarely used, so these salsas are slimming alternatives to heavy bechamel and hollandaise sauces. Most cooked salsas require a large amount or a greater variety of herbs and spices than raw salsas; it is important to learn how to adjust a cooked salsa recipe to taste since fruit and vegetable flavors can vary from one preparation to the next. A blender or food processor is essential in successfully preparing a cooked salsa.

Some salsa recipes combine both raw and cooked ingredients, usually with the raw, texture-enhancing items being added to the cooked salsa. Temperature is of great importance here, so pay close attention to serving directions; a limp, lukewarm salsa can be disastrous.

This book contains a list of exotic ingredients featured in the recipes. Under each heading are notes about ingredients and useful tips to make your salsa preparation easy and creative. Most take minutes to prepare and can be made several hours ahead. Finding this artful marriage of ingredients on your own can take months, even years, as many Mexican cooks will confirm. So use this book as a starting point and an inspiration to achieve your own personal salsa.

I assure you, it is astonishing how many salsa recipes one can eat without growing tired of the flavor of salsa. A change in some of the ingredients or herbs or spices used in a recipe will transform a casual dish into a masterpiece. I urge you to try some of these salsas with your next meal. I wish you luck; there are no rules!

Salsa Ingredients & Techniques

Achiote
Rich orange to brick red colored achiote, or annatto, seeds, used after being ground into a fine powder, add a lovely golden color and earthy flavor to food. Should be used in conjunction with other spices or chili pepper for maximum effect.

Avocados
The bumpy skinned Haas, which turns from green to black when ripe, has a rich, buttery flesh and sweetish flavor. Slick, green skinned Fuerte avocados stay green when ripe and have a more watery consistency and soapy taste. Haas are preferred for these recipes, especially when bought green and allowed to ripen on a sunny windowsill.

Banana
Just about the most popular fresh fruit, widely used for dessert or eaten raw. Bananas are best when they are yellow with a few black spots.

Bean
For recipes in this book, use dried black beans, which need no presoaking and cook up in 1-1/2 hours, or use canned.

Berries
Strawberries, raspberries, blackberries, boysenberries and cranberries are used in recipes in this book. You may have to cut larger berries in half in order to keep them in proportion with other ingredients.

Chayote

A versatile pear-shaped fruit with a smooth to slightly spiny skin. It tastes like a blend of cucumber and squash.

Cheeses

Melting cheeses—Cheddar and Jack—are the most traditional for our recipes.

Chili Peppers

The word chili has been traced back to the Aztec Indians of central Mexico and describes many types of hot peppers used in preparing uncooked and cooked salsas. Varieties in this book include the following:

Anaheim: mild, 2 inches wide at the shoulders and tapering, 6 to 8 inches long, usually glossy green but partly or entirely orange-red when vine ripened. These peppers are also known as New Mexico green chilies but are actually grown in California and are milder than the New Mexico variety. They are sold fresh from spring through autumn, or canned preroasted and skinned, whole or diced, under the generic name "mild green chilies." Anaheims add flavor without much heat. Dried Anaheims are available all year round as whole red pepper ristras (handstrung ropes of chilies), ground into powders, or in preparations such as bottled pastes and sauces.

Ancho: see Poblano.

Arbol: very hot, 2 to 3 inches long, usually sold when mature and red but can be mottled green and red or solid green. This skinny pepper is used to add heat, not flavor.

Caribe: the dried, crushed version of New Mexico red chilies, also known as pizza pepper flakes. This is not a powder.

Cayenne: very hot, bright red: 1/2 inch at the shoulders and about 4 to 6 inches long. When dried, pods and seeds are ground to make a spicy hot pepper of the same name. Lots of heat, virtually no flavor.

Chili Powder: a medium-hot commercial preparation that mixes some or all of the following into a brick-red powder: cayenne, paprika, cumin, salt, cloves, coriander, black pepper, turmeric, and crushed chilies.

Chipotle: see Jalapeño.

Dried Crushed Red Chili Flakes: a commercial preparation usually made from dried red New Mexican or Anaheim chilies. Pieces are individual, rather than ground, with flecks of red, yellow, brown, and even black among the flakes. Pizza parlor pepper flakes are a common example of this type of preparation. Flakes add both heat and flavor, ranging from medium hot to very hot depending on what peppers are used.

Fresno: Also known as a chili caribe or chili cera, these chilies measure about 2 inches in length and between 1 and 1 1/4 inches in length and taper to a rounded end. A wax type chili, thick fleshed, sweet, and hot, they are usually available in the fall. It is sometimes mistaken for a red jalapeño, although the two are different varieties. The fresno is broader at the shoulder and hotter. Excellent in salsas.

Habanero: dangerously hot, 2 to 3 inches long and around, green to golden orange when ripe. These puffy and bloated-looking peppers are a hundred times hotter than the spicy jalapeños; to date, habernos are the hottest peppers on earth. They add much flavor as well as fire power.

Hatch: a variety of the New Mexico green from Hatch, New Mexico, the chili-pepper capital of the world. Can be freely substituted with New Mexico greens.

Hungarian Wax : medium hot, 3 inches long, mild. Let ripen to canary yellow at room temperature before cooking or buy peppers with orange spots. Adds flavor with some heat. Also marketed under the generic name of guero.

Jalapeño: medium hot to very hot, 2 to 3 inches long, deep green to green with red splotches; can be vine-ripened to deep red. This most popular pepper varies in heat depending on the season and where they were grown; a good rule of thumb is to taste a small piece and adjust the recipe accordingly. Adds more heat than flavor, depending on the spiciness of the individual chili. Dried jalapeños are called chipotle; they are medium hot to very hot and brown, with roughly textured skin. These smoked, slightly charred jalapeño peppers add a rich texture and complex flavor to salsas. Jalapeño chilies are usually found canned or bottled rather than sold individually; the reddish brown sauce should be included with the peppers themselves in any recipe use. Adds both flavor and heat.

Mulato: see Poblano.

New Mexico Green: mild to hot, 1 1/2 inches wide at the shoulders, tapers, 4 to 6 inches long, medium green, and glossy. As sweet as the Anaheim but spicier, this is the basic chili pepper for not only salsa but virtually all Mexican and Southwestern cuisine. When ripened late in the season, these chilies turn bright to brick red and are called New Mexico red peppers; they are often dried in bunches.

Pasilla: hot and smoky, 3 inches wide at the shoulders, 5 inches in length, purplish black with wrinkled skin. Also called negro when dried. Often confused with poblano.

Pimiento or Pimento: a plump red pepper about 2 inches wide at the shoulders and almost 4 inches long. Fleshy, very sweet, and sometimes spicy, it is usually cut into strips and pickled along with green olives, although it can be found bottled by itself. When dried and ground, it is called paprika.

Piquin or Peouin: tiny, 1/4 inch in diameter, pellet shaped, orange red to dark reddish brown, and extremely hot. Chilies can be used whole as a flavoring but should be removed prior to serving. Usually used crushed or ground into powder. Substitutes include similarly shaped and incendiary peppers: japones, serrano seco, and arbol.

Poblano: mild to medium hot, 2 to 3 inches wide at the shoulders, tapering, 3 to 5 inches long, and dark green. A type of poblano is marketed in California under the name pasilla. A true poblano is puffier than a pasilla, is shaped like a bell pepper with collapsed sides, and has a sharp tip, while the pasilla has a blunt tip. Adds flavor with some heat and is usually hotter than an Anaheim and milder than a New Mexican green chili or jalapeño.

Poblanos are called ancho or mulato when dried, although anchos are usually deep red in color while mulatos are dark brown to almost black. The skin is dry and extremely wrinkled. Both dried forms have an intense smoky flavor that complements their medium-hot heat. Chilies are sold whole or ground into a brick-red powder.

Serrano: very hot, 1 1/2 to 2 inches long, fairly thin, light to dark green. Often confused with the jalapeño; look for shine, since jalapeños have more sheen. Adds both heat and flavor. Canned peppers are available but are usually pickled and so must be rinsed well before use.

Handling Chilies The flesh of a chili pepper is flavorful but not spicy; the seeds and ribs contain the heat, so remove them for milder salsa. Wear rubber gloves or plastic bags on your hands when handling fresh chili peppers; touching your mouth or eyes with bare fingers during or after the handling of chilies can be painful. If you do develop a burning sensation, immediately flush the affected area with cool water. The spicy aroma of numerous peppers can cause watery eyes or a runny nose, so work in a well-ventilated space, opening windows or switching on a fan to disperse the heavy aromatic scent.

Roasting Chilies Place one or more chilies, as needed, on a grilling rack and broil approximately 4 inches away from heat until the top side is toasty brown (or blackened, as specified in the recipe); turn the pepper over and repeat the process. The skin will blister and split. Before preparing salsa, remove the roasted skin entirely (or partially, as directed) by peeling with fingers (use rubber gloves) under cool water. Some people prefer to place roasted chili peppers inside a sealed plastic bag or in a plastic-covered heat-resistant bowl and let them "sweat" for 15 to 20 minutes prior to removing skins by hand. You can also roast chilies by spearing them on a metal skewer and exposing them to an open flame (gas range, camp fire, miniature propane blowtorch) until the skins darken, then peel as described above.

How to Prepare Dried Chilies Dried chilies must be soaked until they are soft and then pureed. To soften dried chilies, place them in a saucepan, cover with water, and bring to a boil. Remove the saucepan from heat and let the chilies soak in the hot water until softened. The papery peel may remain somewhat stiff, but the pulp will become tender. To puree, remove the stems and seeds. Process the chilies in a blender or food processor with just enough liquid to make a paste. Or use as directed.

How to Prepare Canned Chilies Some canned chilies are packed in oil and some are canned in a marinade called adobo. To remove oils, simply wipe off the oils, or rinse with water and then wipe off. Use as directed.

Warning: The oils of canned chilies can be relentlessly hot; to handle them, wear rubber gloves.

Cilantro
The roundish and lobed leaves of the coriander plant that possess a bold, robust, sagelike flavor with citrus overtones.

Coriander
This term usually refers to the seeds of the coriander plant, which are sold either whole or ground. The fruit are the seeds, which are brownish yellow and lack the sagelike flavor of the leaves, but have a citrus flavor. The leaves are most often called cilantro and are popular as a seasoning and a garnish.

Garlic
A member of the lily family and a relative of onions, shallots, chives, and leeks, it has a strong and pungent flavor, especially

when raw. Frying makes it sweet; when boiled or baked, it becomes mild and creamy.

Guava

A pale green, very aromatic fruit grown in tropical and subtropical areas such as Florida, Cuba, and Hawaii. It is oval shaped with a thick skin, ranges in size from 2 to 4 inches, and has pink or yellow flesh. Seeds, though bothersome, are edible.

Jicama

This large tuberous tropical plant root looks similar to a huge turnip with a tough outer skin that should be peeled off. It is most often used raw in more innovative cooking, especially in salsas where it has a pleasing crunchy texture.

Mango

A sweet fruit of which there are many varieties. It is intensely aromatic when ripe and is used much like a peach. When green, mango is often used in stews or chutneys. Most are grown in Florida, California, and Hawaii. Several recipes in this book use this fruit.

Nopalitos

Nopalitos are the small pads or shoots found on the prickly pear cactus. They have a flavor similar to okra and—like okra—are slightly slimy. They are definitely an acquired taste. Nopalitos, also known as nopales, can be purchased in most Mexican markets. Some markets carry uncooked nopales in plastic bags in the vegetable section, but these are difficult to handle and cook. Precooked nopalitos sold in cans or bottles are easier to use, though you should drain the liquid from the cactus pieces and pat them dry before use.

Oils

The most delicious cooking oils are olive oil, sesame oil, and peanut oil. Extra virgin olive oil is ideal for salsas.

Onions

Yellow, red, white, and green onion are all integral parts of salsa, used either alone or in combination. To vary the flavor of a cooked or uncooked salsa, substitute one variety of onion for another, increasing or decreasing the amount used as desired. Varieties include the following:

Bermuda Onion: medium to large, round with flattened sides, ivory, sweet, available April through June.

Chives: extremely thin, long green stalks, delicate oniony flavor. Substitute for green onions to make salsa less pungent.

Globe Onion: common yellow onion, globular, in various sizes, available year-round.

Green Onion or Scallion: very slim white ends with long, narrow, hollow green stalks, pungent, available year-round. Use the white and green parts in recipes unless instructed otherwise.

Pearl Onion: small, white, oval, sweet, available year-round.

Purple Onion: large, globular, deep red to almost purple, mild, very sweet with pungent overtones, available year-round.

Red Italian Onion: large, globular, red, extremely mild, very sweet, available March through September.

Scallion: see Green Onion.

Shallot: red, lavender, and pale green varieties; lavender is sweeter, never spicy, and adds an elegantly subtle nut flavor to salsa.

Spanish Onion: large, globular, golden brown, mild, sweet, available from September through March.

Peeling Problems Most salsas feature one or more onions. Peeling them can be difficult and time consuming. Try boiling globular onions for two to three minutes; extremely large onions may take one to two minutes more. Drain the boiled onions, then plunge them into a bowl of ice water. This will not only make the skins peel off more easily but will also make the onions less pungent.

Quick Cuts While chopping green onions is easy to do with a sharp knife, I find that using scissors on the green stalks is not only faster but gives more control. Mincing chives with scissors is almost a necessity since pressing down on the tender shoots with a knife bruises them, releasing their vital flavorful juices.

Onion Odor Like chili peppers, onions give off a very strong scent that can induce tearing or sniffing. Make sure the workspace is properly ventilated, opening windows to increase air flow if necessary. If the aroma is still overpowering, try a trick I picked up from watching a photographer loading film in the Arizona sunshine: Peel and prepare the onion inside a large bag! While shutterbugs must use black opaque bags, I use a clear plastic bag (from the dry cleaner). Spread the bag on the counter and open the bottom edge facing you. Slide the cutting board, knife, and onion inside, letting the bag's top surface drape over your forearms and hands. Prepare the onion as usual, and notice how most of the fumes stay inside the bag!

Soap and water are often not powerful enough to remove onion odor. Try wetting your hands with cool water, pouring salt into one palm, and washing your hands with the salt as you would normally. Rinse with plenty of cool water. Finish by applying hand lotion.

Papaya

A sweet, tender melonlike fruit that often has a bright orange flesh. The seeds of the papaya are delicious in salsas. Good raw or in salsas.

Passion Fruit

A small round fruit that resembles a strong brittle-skinned yellow or purple plum with a very aromatic flavor. Its juice is often used in punches, salsas, and sorbets. Do not try to remove the seeds when making salsa, but do remove and discard the skin.

Star Fruit

This oblong fruit with five unusual ridges forms a star shape when cut widthwise. It's about 4 to 5 inches long and 2 inches across. The thin, smooth skin ripens from yellow green to rich golden yellow. The pale yellow flesh is translucent, crisp and juicy, with occasional seeds. The taste can be similar to citrus and ranges from very sweet to somewhat tart.

Tomatoes

Green, red, and yellow tomatoes, plus the little green-skinned husked tomatoes called tomatillos, are all utilized in salsa recipes. Here are some guidelines:

Cherry Tomatoes: sweet, approximately 1 inch in diameter, with lots of juice and seeds. Should be cut into quarters or eighths, then seeded for uncooked salsa unless the fruit is very firm and not runny. For cooked salsa simply cut in half and remove the seeds if specified.

Green Tomatoes: unripe garden-variety tomatoes usually range from 2 to 4 inches in diameter and have an even balance of seeds and juice to meaty ribs. Firmer and less sweet than ripened or red tomatoes, they are not as tart as tomatillos, so they complement many salsa recipes. Used in combination with ripe tomatoes, they add more definition and complex flavor, and should be seeded. Some cooks insist on blanching the tomatoes to remove their skins before making salsa; I consider this unnecessary unless the skin is exceedingly thick. Most store-bought green tomatoes have thin skins.

Plum Tomatoes, Also Known As Italian, Italian Plum, or Roma Tomatoes: red oblong tomatoes about 1 1/2 inches in diameter and 3 inches long. They are very firm when ripe and have fewer seeds and less liquid than other varieties. Their skin is very thin and is not removed when making salsa. Their robust taste and meaty texture make them a wonderful choice for any recipe in this book; simply substitute two plum tomatoes for a medium tomato.

Red Tomatoes: ripe garden-variety tomatoes come in three basic sizes: small (2 inches in diameter), medium (3 inches in diameter), and large (4 inches in diameter). Beefsteak tomatoes, which often reach 6 inches in diameter and can weigh over a pound, aren't the best for salsa—they're too juicy and bland. It is best to buy tomatoes that are almost ripe, then let them ripen naturally on a sunny windowsill for several days before use. Tomatoes should be seeded, although skins do not need to be removed unless the fruit is especially thick-skinned. Use the most flavorful tomatoes you can find even if you have to grow them yourself, for a sensational salsa depends on bold, sweet, tasty tomatoes.

Semi-Ripe Tomatoes: are sometimes found in supermarkets but are mostly a home-grown product. These tomatoes are harvested halfway on their way to ripeness. Not as tart as completely green tomatoes, yet they lack the sweet juiciness of red ones. They are to be considered as a filler rather than a dominant flavor in salsa and should be used only in conjunction with either completely unripe or ripe tomatoes.

Tomatillos, Also Known As Husk Tomatoes: range from 1 1/2 to 2 1/2 inches in diameter and are completely or partially covered in a wrinkly paperlike husk. This husk must be removed and the tomatillo washed thoroughly in soapy water prior to use in order to eliminate the clear, waxy residue that clings to the skin; make sure to rinse well and pat dry. These tart fruits with minuscule seeds do not need to be removed when used in uncooked or cooked salsa. Dice tomatillos as directed for uncooked salsa; halve or quarter each fruit for cooked salsa.

Vinegars

A number of delightfully flavored vinegars can be used in salsa. The recipes in this book use balsamic vinegar, apple cider vinegar, rice vinegar, red wine vinegar, and garlic wine vinegar.

Traditional Salsas

Jamaican Dry Jerk Seasoning

Makes about 1/2 cup

1 tablespoon onion flakes

1 tablespoon onion powder

2 teaspoons ground thyme

1 teaspoon ground cumin

1 teaspoon ground pimento (allspice)

1/4 teaspoon ground nutmeg

1/4 teaspoon ground cinnamon

2 teaspoons sugar

1 teaspoon coarsely ground black pepper

1 1/2 teaspoons cayenne pepper

2 teaspoons dried chives or green onions

Mix all the ingredients together. Store in a tightly closed glass jar. It will keep its pungency for over a month.

This seasoning mix is excellent to have on hand to sprinkle on cooked or uncooked fish, vegetables, or snacks.

**8 servings
(1 tablespoon each)**

Calories: 13

Protein: 0

Carbohydrates: 3 gm

Fat: 0

Fresh Salsa

A good topping on grilled meat or boiled green vegetables.

Makes about 2 1/2 cups

2 medium tomatoes, peeled and
    coarsely chopped

4 scallions, finely chopped

3 serrano chili peppers, finely
    chopped

1 clove garlic, minced

1/4 cup finely chopped cilantro

2 tablespoons lemon juice

1/4 teaspoon ground white pepper

Combine all the ingredients in
a large bowl. Mix well. Cover
the bowl and refrigerate at
least 3 hours before serving.
Use within a week.

**40 servings
(1 tablespoon each)**
Calories: 3
Protein: 0
Carbohydrates: 1 gm
Fat: 0

Salsa Cruda

This salsa is good for dipping and for spooning on eggs, grilled meats, or almost anything.

Makes about 3 cups

3 large ripe red tomatoes, finely diced

3/4 cup chopped cilantro, including some stems

1/2 cup finely diced red onion

1/4 cup fresh lime juice

2 serrano chili peppers, seeded and minced

2 teaspoons minced garlic

Combine all the ingredients in a medium bowl. Mix well. Cover and refrigerate at least 1 hour to blend flavors.

**48 servings
(1 tablespoon each)**
Calories: 4
Protein: 0
Carbohydrates: 1 gm
Fat: 0

Salsa Rossa Cruda

 Use this uncooked salsa as a topping for pasta or boiled rice.

Makes about 2 cups

1 1/2 pounds ripe plum tomatoes, peeled, seeded, and coarsely chopped

1/3 cup coarsely chopped black olives

1/4 cup coarsely chopped fresh basil leaves

1/4 cup extra virgin olive oil

2 small cloves garlic

1/2 cup diced sweet yellow pepper

1/8 teaspoon grated fresh ginger

1/4 teaspoon freshly ground pepper

Combine all the ingredients in a medium bowl. Mix well. Cover and let sit on the countertop 1 1/2 hours to allow flavors to blend before serving.

**32 servings
(1 tablespoon each)**
Calories: 24
Protein: 0
Carbohydrates: 1 gm
Fat: 2 gm

Jalapeño and Tomato Salsa

Use this salsa on grilled or broiled chicken or fish or for a dip with tortilla chips.

Makes about 3 cups

2 cups finely chopped, seeded fresh tomatoes

2 jalapeño chili peppers, seeded and minced

1/3 cup finely chopped red onion

1 teaspoon minced garlic

2 tablespoons minced cilantro

1 teaspoon lime juice

2 teaspoons olive oil

2 cucumbers, peeled and diced

1/8 teaspoon cayenne pepper

1 tablespoon white wine vinegar

Combine all the ingredients in a medium bowl. Mix well. Cover the bowl and refrigerate at least 1 hour before serving.

**48 servings
(1 tablespoon each)**
Calories: 6
Protein: 0
Carbohydrates: 1 gm
Fat: 0

Triple Tomato Salsa

An exciting salsa that can be used on grilled or broiled fish, chicken, and beef. It's also a fine topping for boiled rice or pasta.

Makes about 4 cups

1/2 cup dried tomatoes

1 cup boiling water

3 ripe tomatoes

6 tomatillos, chopped

1 red bell pepper, seeded and chopped

1 jalapeño chili pepper, seeded and chopped

2 scallions, chopped, including some green tops

1/4 cup chopped cilantro

1 tablespoon red wine vinegar

In bowl, mix dried tomatoes and boiling water; soak for 25 minutes. Drain. Finely chop tomatoes and place in medium bowl. Combine remaining ingredients with chopped tomatoes and mix well. Cover the bowl and let sit for 1 hour to allow flavor to blend before serving.

**64 servings
(1 tablespoon each)**

Calories: 4

Protein: 0

Carbohydrates: 1 gm

Fat: 0

Tomato and Fresh Ginger Salsa

Serve it as a topping for grilled skinless, boneless chicken or turkey breasts.

Makes about 1 1/2 cups

2 large tomatoes, seeded and
  chopped

1/4 cup thinly sliced green onions

1/4 cup finely chopped sweet onion

2 tablespoons finely chopped fresh
  ginger

1 teaspoon minced, seeded red
  jalapeño chili pepper

2 tablespoons rice vinegar

1 teaspoon sugar

1 teaspoon fish sauce

Combine all the ingredients in a medium bowl. Mix well to blend. Serve.

Note: Fish sauce is available at Asian markets and in the Asian section of many supermarkets.

**24 servings
(1 tablespoon each)**
Calories: 5
Protein: 0
Carbohydrates: 1 gm
Fat: 0

Spicy Tomato Garlic Salsa

A perfect salsa for tortilla chips or to spoon over your favorite bagels.

Makes about 8 cups

14 1/2- to 16-ounce can stewed tomatoes, well drained

1 medium onion, quartered

10 large cloves garlic, peeled

3 jalapeño chili peppers, stemmed and seeded

1 bunch cilantro, stems trimmed

4 large tomatoes, seeded and quartered

1 sweet yellow pepper, seeded and quartered

6 large green onions, chopped

1 tablespoon Dry Jerk Seasoning (see recipe page 3)

3 tablespoons lemon juice

4 teaspoons lime juice

Combine stewed tomatoes, onion, garlic cloves, jalapeño, and half of cilantro in food processor; process until chunky. Pour mixture into a large bowl. Combine fresh tomatoes, yellow pepper, and remaining cilantro in food processor and process until tomatoes are finely chopped. Add to mixture in large bowl. Mix in the remaining ingredients. Cover the bowl and refrigerate until cold, at least 1 hour or up to 3 hours.

**128 servings
(1 tablespoon each)**
Calories: 3
Protein: 0
Carbohydrates: 1 gm
Fat: 0

Garlic Salsa

Serve this tasty salsa over broiled or poached fish, or spoon over bagels.

Makes about 1 1/2 cups

4 cloves garlic, chopped

2 tomatoes, finely chopped

1/2 cup chopped green onions

2 jalapeño chili peppers, seeded and chopped

1 tablespoon finely chopped cilantro

1 tablespoon lime juice

1/2 teaspoon dried oregano leaves, finely crushed

Pinch cayenne pepper

2 teaspoons olive oil

Combine all ingredients in a medium nonstick skillet and cook over medium heat, stirring occasionally, until hot and bubbly, about 5 minutes. Remove from heat. Serve.

24 servings (1 tablespoon each)

Calories: 7

Protein: 0

Carbohydrates: 1 gm

Fat: 0

Vegetable Salsas

Vegetable Salsa

Serve this salsa with your favorite tortilla chips or use as a topping over a salad of leafy greens.

Makes about 2 1/2 cups

1 carrot, minced

1/2 cup finely chopped jicama

1/2 cup minced red bell pepper

1/2 cup minced red onion

2 tablespoons fresh lemon juice

1 tablespoon minced pickled jalapeño chili pepper

1 tablespoon minced fresh coriander leaves

1/4 teaspoon black pepper

Combine all the ingredients in a medium bowl. Mix well. Cover the bowl and let sit 30 minutes to allow flavor to blend before serving.

**40 servings
(1 tablespoon each)**

Calories: 3

Protein: 0

Carbohydrates: 1 gm

Fat: 0

Garlic Vegetable Salsa

Serve with your favorite tortilla chips or as a condiment.

Makes about 2 1/2 cups

1 celery rib, minced

1 carrot, minced

1/2 cup minced red bell pepper

1/2 cup minced yellow bell pepper

1/2 cup minced red onion

2 tablespoons fresh lemon juice

2 tablespoons minced pickled
    jalapeño chili pepper

1 tablespoon minced fresh coriander
    leaves

1/2 teaspoon minced garlic

Combine all the ingredients in a medium bowl. Mix well. Cover the bowl and let sit 30 minutes to allow flavors to blend before serving.

**40 servings
(1 tablespoon each)**

Calories: 3

Protein: 0

Carbohydrates: 1 gm

Fat: 0

Red Salsa

This salsa is great when it's served over plain cooked black-eyed peas; it's also nice when served over boiled rice or plantains.

Makes about 4 cups

3/4 cup olive oil

1 3/4 cups blanched, peeled, diced tomatoes

4 cloves garlic, diced

1 teaspoon honey

1 teaspoon cayenne pepper

1 teaspoon finely chopped fresh basil

2 teaspoons dried oregano

Freshly ground black pepper

1/3 cup balsamic vinegar

Combine olive oil and tomatoes in a large nonstick skillet. Cook over moderate heat, stirring constantly until softened, about 5 to 10 minutes. Combine next 6 ingredients with tomatoes in skillet. Simmer on low heat, stirring frequently, about 20 to 30 minutes until the sauce has thickened. Remove from the heat. Pour mixture into a medium bowl and stir in the vinegar. Cool or serve hot.

**64 servings
(1 tablespoon each)**
Calories: 24
Protein: 0
Carbohydrates: 1 gm
Fat: 2 gm

Salsa Verde

This salsa goes well with grilled shrimp or chicken, or with potatoes of any kind.

Makes about 2 1/2 cups

12 tomatillos

1/2 cup chopped fresh cilantro

5 cloves garlic, finely chopped

2 jalapeño chili peppers, seeded and minced

1/4 cup lemon juice

1 tablespoon finely chopped scallions

1/2 cup extra virgin olive oil

1 teaspoon small capers

Peel the papery husks off the tomatillos. Rinse the tomatillos, place them in a saucepan, and add water to cover. Bring to a boil and simmer for about 5 minutes or until soft to the touch. Remove the tomatillos from the heat. Lift the tomatillos out of the cooking water, and reserve 1/4 cup of the water. Finely chop the tomatillos and place them in a medium bowl. Add the remaining ingredients. Mix well with the reserved water. Cover and chill a little before serving. Use within a week.

**40 servings
(1 tablespoon each)**

Calories: 28

Protein: 0

Carbohydrates: 1 gm

Fat: 3 gm

Tropical Rainbow Salsa

Serve on grilled or broiled fish or turkey and tortilla chips, too.

Makes about 6 cups

1 large sweet onion, cut into quarters and sliced

1/4 cup balsamic vinegar

2 tomatoes, peeled, seeded, and coarsely chopped

2 yellow tomatoes, peeled, seeded, and coarsely chopped

1 sweet red pepper, seeded and chopped

1 sweet yellow pepper, seeded and chopped

1 green pepper, seeded and chopped

1 clove garlic, finely chopped

1/8 teaspoon cayenne pepper

1/4 cup chopped fresh parsley

1 ripe mango, coarsely chopped

Place onion in a heavy nonstick skillet. Cook onion over medium heat, stirring constantly, until tender and golden brown, adding water if necessary to prevent scorching. Add balsamic vinegar; cook 2 to 3 minutes. Remove mixture from heat. Stir in the tomatoes, peppers, garlic, cayenne, parsley, and mango. Mix well. Pour mixture into a large bowl; cover and refrigerate at least 1 hour before serving.

**96 servings
(1 tablespoon each)**
Calories: 4
Protein: 0
Carbohydrates: 1 gm
Fat: 0

Artichoke Salsa

 This salsa is excellent as a dip for fresh vegetable strips or tortilla chips.

Makes about 1 1/2 cups

16-ounce can artichoke hearts, rinsed well, drained, and chopped

1/4 cup olive oil

1/2 cup finely chopped sweet onion

1 serrano chili pepper, minced

1 clove garlic, minced and mashed to a paste

1 teaspoon minced fresh oregano

In a food processor puree artichoke hearts with oil until very smooth, about 2 minutes. Scrape the puree into a medium bowl and stir in onion, pepper, garlic, and oregano. Mix well. Cover and refrigerate until well chilled, about 4 hours. Use within 3 days.

**24 servings
(1 tablespoon each)**
Calories: 40
Protein: 0
Carbohydrates: 2 gm
Fat: 4 gm

Avocado Salsa

 A good topping on broiled or grilled halibut steak or tilefish.

Makes about 1 1/2 cups

1 firm ripe avocado, diced

2 tablespoons chopped green onion

1 tomato, peeled, seeded, and diced

1 tablespoon chopped fresh basil leaves

1 tablespoon lime juice

1/2 teaspoon grated lime peel

1 tablespoon olive oil

1/8 teaspoon cayenne pepper

Combine all the ingredients in a small bowl. Mix well, stirring gently with a fork to avoid mashing the avocado.

**24 servings
(1 tablespoon each)**
Calories: 19
Protein: 0
Carbohydrates: 1 gm
Fat: 2 gm

Avocado Zucchini Salsa

This salsa is outstanding for tortilla chips or as a topping on grilled or broiled fish steaks.

Makes about 2 cups

3/4 cup finely diced firm but ripe avocado

1/2 cup diced, unpeeled zucchini (about 1/4-inch pieces)

1/4 cup seeded, finely diced plum (Roma) tomato

3 tablespoons finely chopped red onion

3 tablespoons finely chopped cilantro

1 jalapeño chili pepper, seeded and minced

2 teaspoons fresh lime juice

Combine all the ingredients in a medium bowl. Mix well, stirring gently to avoid mashing the avocado. Serve soon or cover and refrigerate. Use within 2 days.

**32 servings
(1 tablespoon each)**
Calories: 8
Protein: 0
Carbohydrates: 1 gm
Fat: 1 gm

Avocado Corn Salsa

A wonderful salsa for grilled or broiled fish fillets and steaks such as salmon, flounder, or swordfish. And don't forget the tortilla chips.

Makes about 2 cups

1/2 cup whole kernel corn

1 ripe avocado, diced

1 scallion, chopped

1/4 cup diced red pepper

1 plum tomato, chopped

1 tablespoon chopped fresh basil leaves

1 tablespoon chopped cilantro

1 jalapeño chili pepper, seeded and minced

2 tablespoons lemon juice

1 tablespoon olive oil

1/8 teaspoon cayenne pepper

In a medium bowl, combine ingredients. Mix well. Let sit 15 minutes to allow flavors to blend before serving.

**32 servings
(1 tablespoon each)**
Calories: 18
Protein: 0
Carbohydrates: 2 gm
Fat: 1 gm

Black Bean Salsa

Serve with tortilla chips or rolled up in flour tortillas.

Makes about 6 1/4 cups

2 15-ounce cans black beans, rinsed and drained

17-ounce can whole kernel corn, drained

2 large tomatoes, seeded and chopped

1 large avocado, chopped

1 purple onion, chopped

1/8 cup chopped fresh parsley

3 to 4 tablespoons lime juice

2 tablespoons olive oil

1 tablespoon red wine vinegar

1/2 teaspoon pepper

Combine all the ingredients in a large bowl. Cover and refrigerate until shortly before serving time. Garnish with avocado slices and fresh parsley, if desired.

**100 servings
(1 tablespoon each)**
Calories: 22
Protein: 1 gm
Carbohydrates: 3 gm
Fat: 1 gm

Corn and Black Bean Salsa

This one goes especially well with broiled or grilled chicken, lean pork chops, or scrambled eggs. It's also perfect by itself rolled up in flour tortillas.

Makes about 4 cups

17-ounce can whole kernel corn, drained

2 Anaheim chili peppers

16-ounce can black beans, rinsed and drained

3 plum tomatoes, chopped

3 tablespoons lemon juice

1/4 teaspoon ground black pepper

1/4 teaspoon ground cumin

Place corn and chili peppers in a shallow baking pan. Broil corn and peppers 5 inches from heat (with electric oven door partially open) 5 to 10 minutes or until charred, stirring occasionally. Cool.

Peel peppers; remove and discard cores and seeds. Combine corn, chili peppers, beans, tomatoes, lemon juice, black pepper, and cumin. Toss to coat. Serve at room temperature.

**64 servings
(1 tablespoon each)**
Calories: 17
Protein: 1 gm
Carbohydrates: 3 gm
Fat: 0

Corn Salsa

This is a great topping over omelets or enchiladas.

Makes about 3 cups

2 cups whole kernel corn

1 red onion, chopped

1 teaspoon minced garlic

1/2 cup diced red bell pepper

1 jalapeño chili pepper, minced

2 tablespoons lime juice

1 tablespoon lemon juice

1 teaspoon olive oil

1 tablespoon chopped cilantro

Combine all ingredients in a medium bowl. Mix well. Cover the bowl and refrigerate at least 1 hour before serving.

**48 servings
(1 tablespoon each)**

Calories: 8

Protein: 0

Carbohydrates: 2 gm

Fat: 0

Corn, Pepper, and Tomato Salsa

 A tasty salsa for tuna steak or your favorite grilled or broiled fish.

Makes about 4 1/2 cups

1 sweet red pepper, seeded and chopped

1 sweet yellow pepper, seeded and chopped

2 17-ounce cans whole kernel corn, drained

2 large tomatoes, seeded and chopped

1 serrano chili pepper, seeded and finely chopped

2 tablespoons ground cumin

1/4 teaspoon ground white pepper

1/4 teaspoon ground oregano

Combine all ingredients in a medium bowl. Mix well. Cover the bowl and refrigerate it at least 1 hour before serving.

**72 servings
(1 tablespoon each)**

Calories: 13

Protein: 0

Carbohydrates: 3 gm

Fat: 0

Spicy Corn Salsa

Serve with fish fillets or grilled or broiled pork chops or as a dip for tortilla chips.

Makes about 2 1/2 cups

10-ounce package frozen whole
    kernel corn, thawed

1 large sweet onion, diced

1 large sweet red pepper, seeded and
    diced

1 clove garlic, minced

2 jalapeño chili peppers, diced

1 tablespoon chopped cilantro

2 tablespoons cider vinegar

1 tablespoon olive oil

1 teaspoon honey

1/8 teaspoon cayenne pepper

Combine all the ingredients in a medium bowl. Mix well. Cover the bowl and refrigerate it at least 1 hour before serving.

**40 servings
(1 tablespoon each)**

Calories: 12

Protein: 0

Carbohydrates: 2 gm

Fat: 0

Corn and Zucchini Salsa

Serve over hot pasta like cavatelli or medium shells or on top of boiled or fried rice.

Makes about 6 cups

2 tablespoons oil

1 cup diced red onions

2/3 cup diced red pepper

2 cups diced zucchini

2 tablespoons minced jalapeño chili pepper

1 clove garlic, minced

1 can (13 1/2 or 14 3/4 ounces) chicken broth

4 cups fresh corn

1/2 cup sour cream

1/4 cup chopped fresh cilantro

1 tablespoon lime juice

Heat oil in a large nonstick skillet over medium heat. Add onions; cook 5 minutes. Add red pepper and zucchini; cook 3 minutes. Add jalapeño, garlic, and broth; bring to boil. Add corn; cook 5 minutes. Remove skillet from heat. Stir in remaining ingredients and mix well. Serve.

**96 servings
(1 tablespoon each)**
Calories: 13
Protein: 0
Carbohydrates: 2 gm
Fat: 1 gm

Lima Corn Salsa

 This tasty salsa for fried green tomatoes is great on fried potatoes or tortilla chips.

Makes about 3 1/2 cups

1 cup frozen baby lima beans, cooked

1 cup frozen whole kernel corn, thawed

1/2 cup diced red bell pepper

3 tablespoons chopped fresh basil

1 fresno chili pepper, seeded and finely chopped

1 tablespoon white wine vinegar

1 teaspoon olive oil

2 cloves garlic, diced

Pinch of cayenne pepper

Combine all the ingredients in a medium bowl. Mix well. Cover the bowl and refrigerate for 1 hour before serving to allow flavors to blend.

**56 servings
(1 tablespoon each)**

Calories: 7

Protein: 0

Carbohydrates: 1 gm

Fat: 0

Eggplant Salsa

This excellent salsa can be served as a side dish with barbecued meat, or a topping for boiled or fried rice.

Makes about 3 cups

1 medium eggplant, pared and sliced 1/4-inch thick

Olive oil

1 cup canned corn, rinsed

3 plum tomatoes, seeded and cut into 1/4-inch cubes

1 poblano chili pepper, roasted until just brown in places and minced

2 green onions, finely diced

2 tablespoons olive oil

2 teaspoons lemon juice

1 teaspoon minced fresh basil leaves

1 teaspoon minced fresh oregano

Brush both sides of the eggplant slices lightly with olive oil. Arrange the slices on a grill rack approximately 6 inches away from the heating element; broil for 3 minutes on each side. Remove from heat and let cool. Cut the eggplant into 1/4-inch cubes and toss with the remaining ingredients in a medium bowl. Mix well. Serve warm or at room temperature, or cover and refrigerate up to 2 days.

**48 servings
(1 tablespoon each)**
Calories: 12
Protein: 0
Carbohydrates: 1 gm
Fat: 1 gm

Gazpacho Salsa

Serve with your favorite tortilla chip, or serve on shredded lettuce as a flavorful salad.

Makes about 5 cups

3 tomatoes, chopped

3 ripe avocados, peeled and chopped

4 green onions, thinly sliced

4-ounce can chopped ripe olives, undrained

3 jalapeño chili peppers, seeded and chopped

2 tablespoons olive oil

1 1/2 tablespoons apple cider vinegar

1 teaspoon minced garlic

1/4 teaspoon black pepper

Combine first 5 ingredients in a large bowl; mix. Combine next 4 ingredients; drizzle over tomato mixture, and toss gently. Cover the bowl and refrigerate for 4 hours before serving. Use within 2 days.

**80 servings
(1 tablespoon each)**
Calories: 17
Protein: 0
Carbohydrates: 1 gm
Fat: 2 gm

Red Bell Pepper & Tomatillo Salsa

This salsa is best served with the simplest of grilled meat or poultry.

Makes about 3 cups

4 medium tomatillos

1 large red bell pepper, cored and seeded

1/2 sweet yellow bell pepper, cored and seeded

1 jalapeño chili pepper, stemmed

1/2 cup chopped fresh parsley leaves

1 1/2 teaspoons red chili flakes

1/4 teaspoon grated fresh ginger

3/4 cup water

Peel the papery husks off the tomatillos. Rinse the tomatillos and pat them dry. Coarsely chop the tomatillos, bell pepper, chili pepper, and parsley in a food processor. Pour chopped ingredients into a medium bowl and add the remaining ingredients. Mix well. Serve soon or cover, refrigerate, and use within 3 days.

48 servings (1 tablespoon each)
Calories: 3
Protein: 0
Carbohydrates: 1 gm
Fat: 0

Roasted Sweet Pepper Salsa

 Serve on shredded lettuce as a salad or
with your favorite tortilla chips.

Makes about 3 cups

1 sweet yellow pepper
1 sweet red pepper
1 sweet green pepper
1/4 cup apple juice
2 tablespoons balsamic vinegar
1 tablespoon Dijon mustard
1 1/2 teaspoons olive oil
1/8 teaspoon cayenne pepper
1/8 teaspoon black pepper

Broil peppers about 2 inches from heat source, turning often, until blackened on all sides. Place in a brown paper bag until cool enough to handle. Remove skin. Core the peppers and remove seeds, then chop the peppers. In a medium size bowl, whisk together the remaining ingredients. Add roasted peppers; mix well to coat. Cover and refrigerate until ready to serve.

**48 servings
(1 tablespoon each)**
Calories: 4
Protein: 0
Carbohydrates: 1 gm
Fat: 0

Sweet Onion Salsa

This salsa can be served with grilled salmon or chicken.

Makes about 2 cups

3/4 cup sliced sweet onion (about 1 pound) cut into 1/4-inch slices

Olive oil flavored vegetable cooking spray

1 cup diced, seeded tomato

2 tablespoons finely chopped fresh basil

1 red jalapeño chili pepper, seeded and finely chopped

2 teaspoons extra virgin olive oil

2 teaspoons white wine vinegar

1/8 teaspoon pepper

Pinch of Dry Jerk Seasoning (see recipe page 3)

Preheat oven to 400°. Arrange onion slices in a single layer on jelly roll pan coated with cooking spray. Bake for 15 minutes. Turn over the onion slices, and bake an additional 20 minutes or until tender and lightly browned. Let cool; coarsely chop onion.

Combine the chopped onion and remaining ingredients in a medium bowl; mix well. Let sit for 20 minutes to allow flavors to blend before serving.

**32 servings
(1 tablespoon each)**
Calories: 5
Protein: 0
Carbohydrates: 1 gm
Fat: 0

Green Tomato Salsa

Goes great on grilled chicken or grilled pork, or marinated and grilled steak. It makes tortilla chips taste exciting.

Makes about 2 cups

1 poblano chili pepper

1 cup finely chopped, seeded green tomatoes

1 jalapeño chili pepper, seeded and minced

2 tablespoons chopped fresh cilantro

1/2 teaspoon ground cumin

2 tablespoons red wine vinegar

1/2 cup diced red onion

Roast the poblano pepper for 8 minutes. Cool. Peel and remove seeds, then chop. Combine with remaining ingredients in a medium bowl. Mix well. Serve.

**32 servings
(1 tablespoon each)**
Calories: 3
Protein: 0
Carbohydrates: 1 gm
Fat: 0

Semi-Ripe Tomato Salsa

 A salsa for pasta or boiled rice.

Makes about 4 cups

1 large sweet onion, chopped

2 teaspoons olive oil

1 cup chicken broth

3 semi-ripe tomatoes, peeled, seeded, and coarsely chopped

1 sweet yellow pepper, seeded and coarsely chopped

2 cloves garlic, diced

Pinch cayenne pepper

Pinch ground oregano

Combine onions and olive oil in a large nonstick skillet and cook over moderate heat just until onions are transparent. Add the remaining ingredients. Cook uncovered until most of the moisture has evaporated and mixture is thick. Remove from heat. Let sit 5 minutes to allow flavors to blend before serving.

**64 servings
(1 tablespoon each)**

Calories: 5

Protein: 0

Carbohydrates: 1 gm

Fat: 0

Poblano Tomato Salsa

 Use this salsa on grilled or broiled chicken, turkey, or pork chops.

Makes about 1 3/4 cups

4 poblano chilies (12 ounces)

1 tablespoon olive oil

1 tablespoon fresh lime juice

1 tablespoon chopped fresh cilantro

1/2 teaspoon ground cumin

1 1/2 cups finely diced plum
   tomatoes

Heat grill or broiler. Grill poblanos, turning until charred all over, 10 to 20 minutes. Place in a brown paper bag until cool enough to handle. Remove skin and seeds. Dice poblano. Combine olive oil, lime juice, cilantro, and cumin in a medium bowl. Add poblanos and tomatoes; toss to coat. Cover and refrigerate up to 4 hours.

**28 servings
(1 tablespoon each)**
Calories: 11
Protein: 0
Carbohydrates: 2 gm
Fat: 0

Tomatillo Salsa

Use on baked, grilled, or broiled fish fillet.

Makes about 2 cups

1/2 pound tomatillos, husked, rinsed, cored, and quartered

2 cloves garlic

1/2 teaspoon mustard seed

1 1/2 tablespoons rice vinegar

1 tablespoon fresh lime juice

1 1/4 teaspoons cayenne pepper

2 teaspoons sugar

1 1/2 teaspoons drained bottled white horseradish

Combine tomatillos, garlic, and mustard seeds in food processor; process until very coarsely chopped. Add the remaining ingredients and process to blend. Pour mixture into a medium bowl. Serve at room temperature.

Note: Do not overprocess tomatillo salsa; overprocessing will make it watery.

**32 servings
(1 tablespoon each)**
Calories: 4
Protein: 0
Carbohydrates: 1 gm
Fat: 0

Zucchini Salsa

This salsa can be eaten with tortilla chips, crackers, or toasted wedges of pita, or over leafy greens as a salad.

Makes about 2 1/2 cups

3/4 cup coarsely chopped fresh plum (Roma) tomatoes

1 cup diced, unpeeled zucchini

1/4 cup chopped scallions, including some green tops

2 tablespoons chopped cilantro

1 tablespoon seeded, minced jalapeño chili pepper

2 tablespoons red wine vinegar

1 teaspoon olive oil

1/4 teaspoon minced garlic

Combine all the ingredients in a medium bowl. Mix well. Cover the bowl and refrigerate at least 2 hours before serving. Use within 2 days.

**44 servings
(1 tablespoon each)**

Calories: 2

Protein: 0

Carbohydrates: 0

Fat: 0

Zucchini and Corn Salsa

This is a great topping on grilled or broiled fish steaks.
Or you could just eat this salsa with tortilla chips.

Makes about 3 1/2 cups

1/2 cup sliced scallions

1 1/2 tablespoons olive oil

2 medium zucchini, peeled and
coarsely chopped

2 cups corn

1 red bell pepper, seeded and
coarsely chopped

1 jalapeño chili pepper, diced

In a nonstick 12-inch skillet,
cook scallions in oil over moderate heat, stirring constantly
until softened. Add the remaining ingredients. Cook
uncovered, stirring constantly
until vegetables are tender,
about 5 minutes. Serve.

**56 servings
(1 tablespoon each)**

Calories: 9

Protein: 0

Carbohydrates: 1 gm

Fat: 0

Fruit Salsas

Fruit Salsa

A good salsa with grilled or broiled chicken, Cornish hens, or turkey.

Makes about 3 cups

2 peaches, seeded and diced

2 kiwis, peeled and diced (1/4-inch pieces)

1 jalapeño chili pepper, seeded and minced

8-ounce can crushed pineapple, drained

1 tablespoon minced cilantro

1/2 teaspoon sugar

1 teaspoon grated lime rind

2 tablespoons lime juice

1/8 teaspoon ground mace

Combine all the ingredients in a medium bowl. Mix well. Cover the bowl and refrigerate it until serving time.

**48 servings
(1 tablespoon each)**

Calories: 7

Protein: 0

Carbohydrates: 2 gm

Fat: 0

Citrus Salsa

Serve as a side dish or as a topping over fried or grilled meat or grilled turkey.

Makes about 3 cups

1 large pink grapefruit, separated into sections

1 naval orange, separated into sections

1/3 cup chopped red onion

2 tablespoons lime juice

1 1/2 teaspoons minced jalapeño chili pepper

With a sharp knife, remove white membranes from grapefruit and orange. Slice the grapefruit and orange sections crosswise into pieces about an inch thick and place them in a medium bowl. Add the remaining ingredients. Mix well. Serve within 1 day.

**48 servings
(1 tablespoon each)**
Calories: 3
Protein: 0
Carbohydrates: 1 gm
Fat: 0

Tequila Fruit Salsa

This salsa enhances chicken, turkey, pork, or fish; it's also a nice topping over leafy greens as a salad.

Makes about 3 1/2 cups

2 pears, diced

1 cup diced strawberries

1 guava, peeled, seeded, and chopped

1/3 cup finely diced jicama

1 tablespoon minced fresh ginger

1 tablespoon chopped fresh cilantro

1 tablespoon tequila

1 tablespoon lime juice

1 teaspoon finely chopped green onion tops

1 jalapeño chili pepper, seeded and minced

Combine all ingredients in a medium bowl; mix well. Serve chilled or at room temperature.

**56 servings
(1 tablespoon each)**

Calories: 6

Protein: 0

Carbohydrates: 1 gm

Fat: 0

Spicy Date Salsa

Serve this as a dip for your favorite tortilla chips and vegetables.

Makes about 2 1/2 cups

8-ounce package chopped, pitted dates

1 cup bottled chili sauce

1 teaspoon finely shredded orange peel

1/2 cup orange juice

1/3 cup finely chopped red onion

1/2 teaspoon minced fresh ginger

1 tablespoon minced serrano chili pepper

Combine all the ingredients in a small nonstick saucepan. Bring to a boil, stirring occasionally, about 10 minutes. Remove from heat and pour in small bowl to cool. Serve chilled or at room temperature.

40 servings
(1 tablespoon each)
Calories: 25
Protein: 0
Carbohydrates: 6 gm
Fat: 0

Spicy Mango Salsa

For a real spicy taste, this salsa is good for grilled or broiled chicken or turkey.

Makes about 3 1/2 cups

2 tablespoons unsalted butter

2 peaches, peeled and chopped

1 mango, peeled and chopped

1/4 cup packed brown sugar

2 cups sweet white wine

1/2 cup whipping cream

1/4 teaspoon cayenne pepper

1/2 teaspoon fresh lime juice

Melt butter in medium non-stick saucepan over medium heat. Add fruit and sugar and cook until fruit softens, stirring frequently, about 15 minutes. Add wine and cook until reduced to sauce consistency, about 20 minutes. Add remaining ingredients, and simmer until reduced to sauce consistency, about 10 minutes. Remove from heat. Set aside and let cool.

**56 servings
(1 tablespoon each)**
Calories: 19
Protein: 0
Carbohydrates: 2 gm
Fat: 1 gm

Hot and Sweet Mango Salsa

 Great with grilled chicken, tuna, salmon, swordfish, or shrimp.

Makes about 2 cups

1 large orange

1 large ripe mango, cut into 1/4-inch
  pieces

1/4 cup flaked sweetened coconut

1/4 cup chopped red onion

1/4 cup chopped fresh cilantro

2 tablespoons minced seeded
  jalapeño chili pepper

1/2 tablespoon grated fresh ginger

2 tablespoons lime juice

1/8 teaspoon cayenne pepper

With a sharp knife, cut peeling and outer white membranes from oranges. Cut between membranes to release segments; dice into 1/4-inch pieces. Combine orange and remaining ingredients in a medium bowl. Mix well. Serve.

**32 servings
(1 tablespoon each)**
Calories: 10
Protein: 0
Carbohydrates: 2 gm
Fat: 0

Grapefruit and Onion Salsa

 This salsa goes perfectly with fish or broiled chicken breast.

Makes about 3 cups

3 small ruby red grapefruits, diced into 1/4-inch pieces, removing any seeds

1/2 cup diced sweet onions

1 fresno chili pepper, seeded and diced

2 tablespoons fresh cilantro leaves, finely chopped

1 tablespoon grated fresh ginger

1/4 teaspoon ground cumin

Combine all the ingredients in a medium bowl. Mix well. Serve soon, or cover, refrigerate, and use within a day.

**48 servings
(1 tablespoon each)**
Calories: 6
Protein: 0
Carbohydrates: 1 gm
Fat: 0

Mango and Cantaloupe Salsa

**Great on grilled or broiled fish, especially salmon
or swordfish steak, or even shrimp kebabs.**

Makes about 3 cups

1 cup diced mango

1 cup diced cantaloupe

4 1/2-ounce can chopped green
   chilies, drained

1/3 cup thinly sliced scallions

1 tablespoon grated fresh ginger

1/4 cup chopped cilantro

2 tablespoons lime juice

1/8 teaspoon cayenne pepper

Combine all ingredients in a
medium bowl. Toss to mix
well. Serve soon or cover and
refrigerate up to 3 days.

**48 servings
(1 tablespoon each)**
Calories: 5
Protein: 0
Carbohydrates: 1 gm
Fat: 0

Mango and Papaya Salsa

 This salsa is good for grilled or broiled chicken, beef, and fish and for topping leafy greens for a salad.

Makes about 2 cups

1 ripe mango, diced

1 ripe papaya, seeded and diced

3 green onions, chopped

3 tablespoons chopped fresh cilantro

1 tablespoon lemon juice

1 cup diced fresh pineapple

2 tablespoons seeded, chopped fresh
    jalapeño

1 teaspoon minced garlic

Combine all ingredients in a medium bowl. Toss to mix well. Cover and refrigerate until about an hour before serving time.

**32 servings
(1 tablespoon each)**

Calories: 11

Protein: 0

Carbohydrates: 3 gm

Fat: 0

Mango Jalapeño Salsa

**For grilled or broiled chicken, tuna, salmon,
or shrimp, this salsa is the one.**

Makes about 2 cups

2 ripe mangos, diced

1 jalapeño chili pepper, seeded and
    minced

2 tablespoons coarsely chopped
    cilantro leaves

1 tablespoon lime juice

1/2 teaspoon grated ginger

1/8 teaspoon crushed cardamom

Combine all the ingredients in
a medium bowl. Mix well.
Cover and refrigerate until
about 1 hour before serving
time.

**32 servings
(1 tablespoon each)**
Calories: 9
Protein: 0
Carbohydrates: 2 gm
Fat: 0

Hot Melon Salsa

It's perfect for rolling up in flour tortillas, as a filling for pita pockets, or serving on shredded lettuce as a salad.

Makes about 3 cups

1 cup seeded and cubed honeydew melon

1 cup seeded and cubed cantaloupe

1 cup seeded and cubed watermelon

1 green jalapeño chili pepper, seeded and finely chopped

1 red jalapeño chili pepper, seeded and finely chopped

1 tablespoon honey

Pinch cayenne pepper

2 tablespoons lime juice

1/4 cup finely chopped fresh basil

Combine all the ingredients in a medium bowl. Mix well. Cover the bowl and refrigerate at least 3 hours.

**48 servings
(1 tablespoon each)**
Calories: 5 gm
Protein: 0
Carbohydrates: 1 gm
Fat: 0

Orange Salsa

 Fruit-based condiments are increasing in popularity; serve this delicious accompaniment with almost any broiled or grilled fish.

Makes about 1 1/2 cups

2 navel oranges, peeled and sepa-
    rated into sections
1/3 cup finely chopped red onion
2 teaspoons olive oil
1 1/2 teaspoons minced garlic
1/4 teaspoon cumin
1/4 teaspoon ground turmeric
1/8 teaspoon cayenne pepper
1 tablespoon grated fresh ginger
1/4 cup chopped fresh coriander

Slice the orange sections cross-wise into pieces about an inch thick, and place them in a small bowl. Add the onion, olive oil, garlic, cumin, turmeric, cayenne pepper, and ginger to the oranges, stirring the ingredients to combine them well. Cover the bowl and refrigerate the salsa until shortly before serving time.

Before serving the salsa, stir in the coriander.

**24 servings
(1 tablespoon each)**
Calories: 10
Protein: 0
Carbohydrates: 2 gm
Fat: 0

Orange and Onion Salsa

 A delicious accompaniment to a grilled or broiled fish steak such as salmon, swordfish, and tuna.

Makes about 3 cups

2 oranges, diced into 1/4-inch pieces, removing any seeds

1/2 cup chopped sweet onions

1 fresno chili pepper, seeded and chopped

2 tablespoons fresh cilantro leaves, finely chopped

1 tablespoon grated fresh ginger

1/4 teaspoon ground cumin

Combine all the ingredients in a medium bowl. Mix well. Serve right away, or cover and refrigerate. Use within a day.

48 servings (1 tablespoon each)

Calories: 4

Protein: 0

Carbohydrates: 1 gm

Fat: 0

Orange Craisin Salsa

Enjoy this salsa over fried duck or chicken, or grilled chicken or turkey. Also spoon over boiled rice.

Makes about 2 1/2 cups

3 seedless oranges
1 cup sake or dry Riesling
1/3 cup seasoned rice vinegar
1/3 cup chicken broth
1/3 cup craisins (dried cranberries)
3 tablespoons honey
2 teaspoons minced fresh ginger
1 tablespoon cornstarch
1 tablespoon minced parsley
1/4 teaspoon ground cumin

With a sharp knife, cut peeling and outer white membranes from oranges. Cut between membranes to release segments; dice into 1/4-inch pieces. Set aside. In a medium nonstick saucepan combine next 7 ingredients. Bring mixture to a low boil, stirring occasionally, until sauce is reduced to 1 1/2 cups, about 5 minutes. Stir in the parsley, oranges, and cumin. Remove from heat. Pour mixture into a medium bowl. Cover and let sit 5 minutes to allow flavors to blend before serving.

40 servings
(1 tablespoon each)
Calories: 20
Protein: 0
Carbohydrates: 4 gm
Fat: 0

Passion Fruit Salsa

This salsa is a perfect complement to grilled poultry or barbecued pork, or spoon it over pancakes and waffles.

Makes about 1 1/2 cups

1/4 cup orange juice

3 tablespoons sugar

15 dried apricots (about 3 ounces)

1 passion fruit

1 1/4 cups water

1/4 cup craisins (dried cranberries), diced

Combine the first 3 ingredients in a small nonstick saucepan and set aside. Cut passion fruit in half crosswise; scoop out pulp and seeds. Using the back of a spoon, press the pulp through a sieve to remove the seeds. Stir the passion fruit into the apricot mixture and bring mixture to a boil. Reduce heat and simmer, uncovered, for about 10 minutes. Remove from heat and let cool. Pour mixture into food processor and process until smooth. Add water and process until well blended. Pour mixture into a medium bowl. Add craisins and mix well. Cover and refrigerate until serving time.

**24 servings
(1 tablespoon each)**
Calories: 19
Protein: 0
Carbohydrates: 5 gm
Fat: 0

Peach Salsa

Serve this salsa with pork chops or grilled or broiled chicken, or serve with your favorite tortilla chips.

Makes about 4 cups

3 ripe peaches, cut into small chunks

1/2 cup diced green bell pepper

2 large scallions, trimmed and chopped

1/3 cup finely chopped red onion

1 jalapeño chili pepper, seeded and minced

2 tablespoons honey

2 tablespoons lemon juice

1 teaspoon grated lemon peel

1 teaspoon grated fresh ginger

Combine all the ingredients in a medium bowl. Mix well. Cover the bowl and refrigerate it at least 1 hour before serving.

**64 servings
(1 tablespoon each)**
Calories: 5
Protein: 0
Carbohydrates: 1 gm
Fat: 0

Pear Lime Salsa

This salsa is delightful with roasted rabbit or any poultry.

Makes about 2 cups

2 green onions, white part only, finely chopped

1 poblano chili pepper, seeded and minced

2 ripe pears, cored and diced small

2 tablespoons lime juice

1/2 teaspoon grated fresh ginger

1/8 teaspoon cayenne pepper

In a medium bowl, mix all the ingredients together. Serve right away. Pears are fragile and this salsa will not last overnight.

**32 servings
(1 tablespoon each)**

Calories: 7

Protein: 0

Carbohydrates: 2 gm

Fat: 0

Strawberry Kiwi Cranberry Salsa

This is a great topping for bagels or toast. It's also good on grilled or broiled fish, steak, turkey, and chicken, and it's a tasty dip with tortilla chips.

Makes about 4 1/2 cups

1 cup frozen unsweetened whole strawberries, thawed

16-ounce can whole berry cranberry sauce

2 ripe kiwis, peeled and cut into 1/4-inch pieces

1 teaspoon grated orange rind

1 teaspoon grated ginger

1 serrano chili pepper, seeded and cut into chunks

2 tablespoons honey

1 tablespoon lime juice

1/8 teaspoon ground mace

3 tablespoons finely chopped red onion

Combine all the ingredients except the onion in a blender or food processor; process on low speed until smooth. Pour mixture into a medium bowl. Add the onion and mix well. Cover the bowl and refrigerate it at least 1 hour before serving. Serve chilled or at room temperature.

**72 servings
(1 tablespoon each)**
Calories: 14
Protein: 0
Carbohydrates: 4 gm
Fat: 0

Extra Hot Salsas

Spicy Hot Tomato Salsa

This will put new life in your tongue; serve on corn tortilla chips of your choice.

Makes about 3 cups

3 cups finely diced plum tomatoes

1/2 cup minced onion

2 tablespoons lime juice

1 teaspoon olive oil

1 poblano chili pepper, seeded and finely chopped

1/4 teaspoon cayenne pepper

1/2 teaspoon ground black pepper

1 clove garlic, finely chopped

Combine all the ingredients in medium bowl. Mix well. Serve soon or cover, refrigerate, and use within one day.

**48 servings
(1 tablespoon each)**

Calories: 5

Protein: 0

Carbohydrates: 1 gm

Fat: 0

Chipotle and Red Pepper Salsa

 Serve as a dip or as a sauce for grilled meats.

Makes about 1 1/2 cups

1 onion, sliced 1/2-inch thick

2 cloves garlic, minced

1 cup canned roasted red peppers

5 dried (soaked) or canned chipotle chilies (rinsed) (see "How to Prepare Dried Chilies or Canned Chilies," page xv)

2 tablespoons lime juice

In a medium nonstick saucepan, cook onion and garlic over high heat, turning occasionally, until flecked with dark brown, about 8 minutes. Combine half of the onion mixture and half of the red peppers, along with the chilies and lime juice, in a blender or food processor. Process until smooth. Chop remaining onion and red peppers and stir into puree. Serve.

**24 servings
(1 tablespoon each)**
Calories: 5
Protein: 0
Carbohydrates: 1 gm
Fat: 0

Red Hot Chili Garlic Salsa

 Spoon over meat loaf or broiled or grilled turkey.

Makes about 1/2 cup

6 cloves garlic, minced

10 serrano chili peppers, preferably red, seeded and chopped

6 yellow wax chili peppers, seeded and chopped

1/8 teaspoon ground cumin

2 tablespoons lemon juice

1/2 tablespoon olive oil

Combine all ingredients in a medium bowl. Mix well. Serve soon or cover, refrigerate, and use within a day.

**8 servings
(1 tablespoon each)**

Calories: 48

Protein: 2 gm

Carbohydrates: 9 gm

Fat: 1 gm

Sun-Dried Tomato Cheese Salsa

 This salsa is perfect for a party as a dip with tortilla chips, or spoon over baked potatoes, omelets, or bagels.

Makes about 2 cups

1/2 ounce sun-dried tomatoes, packed without oil (about 6)

1 cup boiling water

1 tablespoon butter or margarine

1 medium yellow onion, finely diced

3 cloves garlic, minced

1 tablespoon all-purpose flour

1/2 cup tomato juice

2 serrano chili peppers, seeded and minced

1/4 red bell pepper, seeded and finely chopped

1/2 teaspoon crushed red pepper flakes

1 tablespoon minced cilantro

1/2 teaspoon cayenne pepper

3/4 cup shredded sharp cheddar cheese

3/4 cup shredded hot pepper Monterey Jack cheese

Combine sun-dried tomatoes and boiling water in a small bowl; let stand for 30 minutes. Drain and chop. Set aside.

Melt butter in a large nonstick saucepan over medium heat. Add onion and garlic and cook until softened, stirring frequently, about 4 minutes. Stir in flour. Cook about 2 minutes. Pour in tomato juice slowly, stirring until smooth and slightly thickened. Add sun-dried tomatoes and the remaining ingredients. Simmer, stirring frequently, until cheeses melt. Remove from heat and pour mixture into a medium bowl; serve immediately.

**32 servings
(1 tablespoon each)**
Calories: 30
Protein: 2 gm
Carbohydrates: 2 gm
Fat: 2 gm

Sour Cream Salsa

Serve over steamed vegetables, with a plain pasta side dish, or over a green leaf salad.

Makes about 2 1/2 cups

2 jalapeño chili peppers, seeded and diced

1 serrano chili pepper, seeded and diced

1 yellow wax chili pepper, seeded and diced

2 radishes, chopped

2 cloves garlic, chopped

3 scallions, chopped

2 medium tomatoes, seeded and chopped

1 cup cilantro leaves

1 tablespoon tomato paste

1/2 cup water

2 tablespoons olive oil

3/4 cup sour cream

Combine all the ingredients except the oil and sour cream in a food processor or blender. Process until smooth. In a medium nonstick skillet, heat oil over medium to low heat. Transfer the contents of the food processor into the skillet and cook for about 5 minutes or until thickened. Remove from the heat and immediately stir in the sour cream, mixing well until there are no lumps. Serve right away, or cover, refrigerate, and use within 3 days.

**40 servings
(1 tablespoon each)**
Calories: 18
Protein: 0
Carbohydrates: 1 gm
Fat: 2 gm

Garlic Cheese Salsa

 This salsa can be used on baked or mashed potatoes, French fries, boiled or fried rice, or as a dip with tortilla chips.

Makes about 3 cups

2 teaspoons olive oil

1 cup finely diced yellow onion

2 cloves garlic, minced

2 guero chili peppers, seeded and minced

2 jalapeño chili peppers, seeded and minced

14-ounce can peeled tomatoes, chopped into 1/4-inch pieces, with juice reserved

1 tablespoon ground oregano

1 tablespoon minced cilantro

1 teaspoon sugar

1/2 teaspoon garlic powder

1/2 teaspoon cayenne pepper

1 cup shredded hot pepper Monterey Jack cheese

1 cup shredded sharp cheddar cheese

1/2 cup sour cream

In a large nonstick saucepan, heat oil over medium heat. Add onion and garlic. Cook until tender, but not browned, about 1 minute. Add chilies and tomatoes; reduce heat. Add the next 7 ingredients. Cover and stir frequently until cheese is melted. Stir in sour cream. Cook just until heated (do not boil), about 2 minutes. Remove from heat and pour mixture into a medium bowl; serve hot or at room temperature.

**48 servings
(1 tablespoon each)**
Calories: 30
Protein: 1 gm
Carbohydrates: 1 gm
Fat: 2 gm

Wild Combinations

Cool Down Salsa

This salsa makes a great partner for roasted meat, grilled fish, or chicken.

Makes about 3 1/2 cups

1 red jalapeño chili pepper, seeded and finely chopped

1/4 cup finely chopped red onion

1 cup chopped, unpeeled zucchini

Juice of 2 limes

1 cup coarsely chopped cantaloupe

1 cup diced pear

2 tablespoons chopped fresh parsley leaf

Combine jalapeño, onion, and zucchini in a medium bowl. Squeeze juice from both limes into bowl. Add the remaining ingredients and mix well. Cover the bowl and refrigerate at least 1 hour before serving.

**56 servings
(1 tablespoon each)**

Calories: 4

Protein: 0

Carbohydrates: 1 gm

Fat: 0

Apple Salsa

Serve over pork loin roast, pork steak, turkey, or corn tortilla chips.

Makes about 6 cups

4 tart apples, such as Granny Smith or Gala, cored and diced

1 red onion, diced

1 red bell pepper, diced

1 jalapeño chili pepper, minced

1/3 cup dried currants

1 tablespoon finely chopped cilantro

1 teaspoon finely grated fresh ginger

3/4 cup fresh orange juice

2 tablespoons Dijon mustard

1 tablespoon ground cumin

1/2 cup safflower oil

1 tablespoon dark sesame oil

Combine the first seven ingredients in a large bowl. Combine orange juice, mustard, and cumin in a food processor or blender. Process until smooth. With the machine on, gradually add the safflower oil, then the sesame oil, in a very thin stream; the dressing will thicken. Pour the dressing over the apple mixture. Toss gently to mix well. Cover and refrigerate for 2 to 4 hours before serving.

**96 servings
(1 tablespoon each)**
Calories: 18
Protein: 0
Carbohydrates: 2 gm
Fat: 1 gm

Banana Salsa

This topping is great for baked fish fillets or grilled chicken or used as a dip for finger vegetables.

Makes about 4 cups

2 ripe bananas, chopped

1/2 cup chopped sweet red bell pepper

1/2 cup chopped sweet yellow bell pepper

3 green onions, chopped

1 clove garlic, minced

1 1/2 tablespoons honey

3 tablespoons lime juice

1 tablespoon minced cilantro

1 tablespoon sesame oil

1/2 teaspoon ground mace

1 jalapeño chili pepper, seeded and minced

Very gently combine the bananas, bell peppers, onions, and garlic in a medium bowl. Combine the remaining ingredients in a small bowl; mix well. Pour the liquid over the banana mixture and toss gently to coat. Cover and refrigerate at least 3 hours.

**64 servings
(1 tablespoon each)**

Calories: 8

Protein: 0

Carbohydrates: 2 gm

Fat: 0

Spicy Apple Banana Papaya Salsa

A lovely topping over pancakes, French toast, waffles, bagels, or boiled rice.

Makes about 5 cups

6 habanero chili peppers, preferably yellow or red, cut into halves (but not seeded)

1 large yellow onion, chopped (about 2 cups)

1 1/2 cups fresh pineapple, diced into 1-inch cubes

4 tablespoons pure pineapple juice

1 1/2 teaspoons turmeric

1/2 teaspoon ground coriander seed

1/2 teaspoon mace

1/2 teaspoon ground cayenne pepper

1 tablespoon cumin seed

1 teaspoon ground red chili powder

1 1/2 teaspoons ground black pepper

1-inch piece gingerroot, minced

1/4 teaspoon cornstarch

4 tablespoons cider vinegar

2 teaspoons honey

2 green tip bananas, cut into 1/2-inch cubes

1 ripe papaya, cut into 1/2-inch cubes

1 1/2 cups coarsely chopped fresh pineapple

1 golden apple, coarsely chopped

1 red apple, coarsely chopped

6 tablespoons lime juice

1 small red onion, finely chopped

1 clove garlic, finely minced

Place the chili peppers, onion, pineapple juice, spices, and gingerroot in food processor and process until very smooth. In a nonstick large saucepan over low heat, dissolve cornstarch in the vinegar. Add the puree and honey and simmer slowly for 10 minutes. In a large bowl, combine the bananas, papaya, pineapple, apples, lime juice, onion, and garlic. Stir until well coated with lime juice. Add fruit mixture to puree, then simmer 5 minutes over low heat. Remove from heat. Cool and pour in bowl; cover and refrigerate at least 30 minutes. Serve chilled or at room temperature.

**80 servings
(1 tablespoon each)**
Calories: 13
Protein: 0
Carbohydrates: 3 gm
Fat: 0

Papaya and Jalapeño Salsa

**Spoon over grilled chicken or turkey
or over leafy greens as a salad.**

Makes about 2 cups

2 ripe papayas, diced

1 1/4 cups heavy cream

1/4 cup dry sherry

2 tablespoons seeded, finely chopped
    jalapeño chili pepper

1 teaspoon dried tarragon leaves

1 teaspoon white pepper

Puree the papaya and press
through a strainer; set aside.
In a nonstick saucepan over
medium heat, simmer the
heavy cream until it has been
reduced to about 3/4 cup. Add
the papaya. Stir in the
remaining ingredients. Cook
over low heat for 5 minutes.
Remove the pan from the
heat. Cool the salsa to room
temperature. Strain before
serving.

**32 servings
(1 tablespoon each)**
Calories: 41
Protein: 0
Carbohydrates: 2 gm
Fat: 3 gm

Papaya Kiwi Salsa

This salsa is the topping to use for a salad of leafy greens.

Makes about 3 cups

1 firm ripe papaya, seeded and diced

1 kiwifruit, peeled and diced

3 tablespoons lemon juice

2 tablespoons lime juice

1 yellow bell pepper, seeded and diced

1 green bell pepper, seeded and diced

2 jalapeño chili peppers, seeded and diced

1 tablespoon sugar

1 teaspoon grated fresh ginger

Combine all the ingredients in medium bowl. Mix gently. Serve right away or cover and refrigerate it until serving time. Use within 3 days.

**48 servings
(1 tablespoon each)**

Calories: 6

Protein: 0

Carbohydrates: 2 gm

Fat: 0

Watermelon and Papaya Salsa

 This salsa can be served with your favorite tortilla chips or spoon onto your favorite bagels.

Makes about 3 1/2 cups

1 ripe papaya, seeded and diced

2 cups finely diced watermelon

1/2 cup diced, unpeeled zucchini

1/4 cup diced red onion

3 tablespoons lime juice

1 tablespoon diced, seeded jalapeño chili pepper

2 tablespoons chopped fresh cilantro

2 teaspoons olive oil

Combine all ingredients in a medium bowl. Toss to mix well. Serve soon or cover and refrigerate up to 3 days.

**56 servings
(1 tablespoon each)**
Calories: 6
Protein: 0
Carbohydrates: 1 gm
Fat: 0

Melony Rose Fruit Salsa

 This salsa is the perfect complement to rich, highly seasoned crab cakes or fish fillets.

Makes about 4 cups

1 cup diced cantaloupe

1 cup diced watermelon

1 cup diced peeled cucumber

4 ripe plum tomatoes, seeded and diced (1/4-inch pieces)

1/3 cup finely chopped red onion

2 tablespoons fresh lime juice

2 tablespoons coarsely chopped fresh coriander leaves

1/2 teaspoon minced fresh ginger

1 teaspoon minced seeded jalapeño chili pepper

Combine all the ingredients in a medium bowl. Mix well. Cover and let sit at room temperature for up to 1 hour before serving.

**64 servings
(1 tablespoon each)**

Calories: 4

Protein: 0

Carbohydrates: 1 gm

Fat: 0

Melon Mango Salsa

This salsa can punch up the flavor of grilled chicken, beef or fish; it's also good with tortilla chips.

Makes about 4 cups

1 1/2 cups finely diced jicama

1 cup finely diced cantaloupe

1 cup finely diced watermelon

1 ripe mango, diced

2 tablespoons chopped basil

1 tablespoon minced shallot

1/2 teaspoon finely grated fresh ginger

1/4 teaspoon crushed red pepper flakes

3 tablespoons fresh lime juice

Combine all the ingredients in a large bowl. Mix well. Cover the bowl and refrigerate at least 1 hour before serving. Use within 2 days.

**64 servings
(1 tablespoon each)**

Calories: 5

Protein: 0

Carbohydrates: 1 gm

Fat: 0

Chunky Watermelon Salsa

This salsa is the ideal accompaniment for grilled shrimp or chicken.

Makes about 2 cups

1 lime

2 cups diced watermelon (1/2- inch cubes)

1 cup diced jicama (1/4-inch cubes)

1/4 cup thinly sliced green onions

2 tablespoons minced fresh cilantro

2 teaspoons minced, seeded jalapeño chili pepper

1 teaspoon honey

With a small sharp knife, cut peeling and outer white membranes from lime. Cut between membranes to release segments; cut into 1/4-inch pieces. Combine lime and remaining ingredients in a medium bowl. Mix well. Cover and refrigerate for at least 30 minutes before serving. Use within a day.

**32 servings
(1 tablespoon each)**
Calories: 6
Protein: 0
Carbohydrates: 1 gm
Fat: 0

Fruit and Ginger Salsa

 Serve this salsa with grilled or broiled fish steaks
or on corn tortilla chips.

Makes about 2 1/2 cups

1 cup peeled, finely chopped mango

1/2 cup finely chopped fresh
pineapple

1/4 cup finely chopped green bell
pepper

1/4 cup finely chopped red bell
pepper

3 tablespoons thinly sliced green
onions

3 tablespoons chopped fresh
watercress

1/4 teaspoon dry mustard

1/4 teaspoon grated fresh ginger

2 teaspoons balsamic vinegar

2 teaspoons fresh lime juice

Combine all the ingredients in
a medium bowl. Mix well.
Cover and refrigerate until
serving time.

**40 servings
(1 tablespoon each)**

Calories: 4

Protein: 0

Carbohydrates: 1 gm

Fat: 0

Cranberry Salsa

It is terrific with ham, roast turkey, grilled chicken, and pork.

Makes about 2 cups

16-ounce can whole berry cranberry
    sauce

1 cup diced jicama

1/4 cup chopped cilantro

2 teaspoons minced pickled jalapeño
    pepper

2 teaspoons cider vinegar

Combine all the ingredients in a medium bowl. Mix well. Cover the bowl and refrigerate it until serving time. Use within a week.

**32 servings
(1 tablespoon each)**
Calories: 23
Protein: 0
Carbohydrates: 6 gm
Fat: 0

Rhubarb Salsa

A tasty salsa served over chicken or turkey, or as a topping over leafy greens as a salad.

Makes about 4 cups

1 cup sugar

1/4 cup water

1 tablespoon finely shredded orange peel

6 cups rhubarb, sliced 1/2-inch thick

1/2 cup diced green bell pepper

1/4 cup finely chopped sweet onion

1/3 cup finely chopped red onion

1 jalapeño chili pepper, seeded and minced

2 tablespoons honey

2 tablespoons lemon juice

1 teaspoon grated fresh ginger

In a medium nonstick saucepan, combine sugar, water, and orange peel. Bring to a boil over high heat. Add rhubarb; reduce heat. Simmer gently until the rhubarb is very tender, about 20 minutes. Let cool to room temperature. Pour mixture in food processor and process until smooth. Scrape the puree into a large bowl and add the remaining ingredients. Mix well. Serve at room temperature or chilled.

**64 servings
(1 tablespoon each)**
Calories: 17
Protein: 0
Carbohydrates: 4 gm
Fat: 0

Rhubarb Cranberry Ginger Salsa

This makes a nice topping for fruit salads or a syrup for pancakes or waffles, or serve over chicken or turkey.

Makes about 5 cups

1/2 cup sugar

3/4 cup water

1 1/2 tablespoons grated orange peel

4 cups rhubarb, sliced 1/2-inch thick

12-ounce package cranberries

1/2 teaspoon ground ginger

1/4 teaspoon ground mace

1/2 cup pure maple syrup

2 tablespoons finely chopped crystal-lized ginger

1/2 cup chopped craisins (dried cranberries)

1 jalapeño chili pepper, seeded and minced

In a medium nonstick saucepan, combine sugar, water, and orange peel. Bring to a boil over high heat. Add rhubarb; reduce heat. Simmer gently until the rhubarb is very tender, about 20 minutes. Add the next three ingredients and cook until most of the cranberries pop and the mixture thickens slightly, stirring frequently, about 5 minutes. Let sauce cool to room temperature.

Transfer sauce to food processor. Add maple syrup and process until almost smooth. Transfer sauce to medium bowl. Stir in remaining ingredients. Cover the bowl and refrigerate overnight. Serve.

**80 Servings
(1 tablespoon each)**
Calories: 17
Protein: 0
Carbohydrates: 4 gm
Fat: 0

Cranberry and Pickled Beet Salsa

Serve over poultry, beef, or game.

Makes about 3 cups

1/2 cup red wine vinegar

1/2 cup water

2/3 cup sugar

12-ounce bag fresh (picked over) or frozen cranberries

16-ounce jar sliced pickled beets, drained and quartered

1 teaspoon minced pickled jalapeño chili pepper

Combine vinegar, water, and sugar in medium nonstick saucepan. Bring to a boil, stirring to dissolve sugar. Add cranberries and simmer, stirring occasionally, about 20 minutes, or until thick. Stir in beets and pepper. Remove from heat and pour into medium bowl; let cool. Serve chilled or at room temperature.

**48 servings
(1 tablespoon each)**
Calories: 28
Protein: 0
Carbohydrates: 7 gm
Fat: 0

Apple Avocado Salsa

Lovely for a fajita filling along with beef, pork, or chicken.
Makes a good topping for tortilla chips, too.

Makes about 2 cups

1 cup diced Granny Smith apple

1/2 cup diced ripe avocado

1/4 cup diced red bell pepper

1/4 cup diced red onion

1 tablespoon chopped fresh cilantro

1 1/2 teaspoons minced jalapeño chili
    pepper

1/2 teaspoon grated lime rind

1 1/2 tablespoons fresh lime juice

Dash of pepper

1 small clove garlic, minced

Combine all the ingredients in a medium bowl. Mix well. Cover the bowl and refrigerate at least 30 minutes before serving.

**32 servings
(1 tablespoon each)**
Calories: 8
Protein: 0
Carbohydrates: 1 gm
Fat: 0

Tomato Orange Salsa

Serve over grilled or broiled fish steaks like swordfish.

Makes about 3 1/2 cups

2 oranges, peeled and separated into sections

1 1/2 cups chopped seeded tomatoes

1/4 cup minced red onion

1 teaspoon minced red jalapeño chili pepper

1/4 cup chopped cilantro leaves

2 tablespoons orange juice

2 teaspoons minced garlic

2 teaspoons balsamic vinegar

1 teaspoon minced fresh ginger

1/4 teaspoon ground turmeric

1/8 teaspoon cayenne pepper

Use a small, sharp knife to remove the membrane between the orange sections. Slice the orange sections crosswise into pieces about 1/2-inch thick and place them in a medium bowl. Add the remaining ingredients. Mix well. Serve.

56 servings (1 tablespoon each)
Calories: 4
Protein: 0
Carbohydrates: 1 gm
Fat: 0

Citrus Jicama Salsa

Serve with grilled shrimp or poultry, toss with greens, or serve as a dip with your favorite tortilla chips.

Makes about 4 1/2 cups

1 red grapefruit, peeled and separated into sections

1 orange, peeled and separated into sections

2 tablespoons lime juice

1/4 cup finely diced red onion

1/4 teaspoon Dry Jerk Seasoning (see recipe page 3)

1 teaspoon grated fresh ginger

1 cup finely diced jicama

1 teaspoon minced serrano chili pepper

1 teaspoon olive oil

With a sharp knife, remove white membrane from grapefruit and orange. Slice the grapefruit and orange sections crosswise into pieces about 1/2-inch thick and place them in a medium bowl. Add the remaining ingredients. Mix well. Cover the bowl and refrigerate at least 1/2 hour before serving. Serve chilled or at room temperature.

**72 servings
(1 tablespoon each)**
Calories: 3
Protein: 0
Carbohydrates: 1 gm
Fat: 0

Jicama Apple Salsa

This salsa is a savory side dish for pork roast or baked poultry, or serve it alongside scrambled eggs and sausage for a hearty winter breakfast.

Makes about 2 cups

3 tablespoons unsalted butter

1/4 cup finely diced red onion

1 Anaheim chili pepper, roasted, skinned, seeded, and finely diced

1 medium jicama, cut into 1/4-inch cubes

1 large tart green apple, peeled and cut into 1/4-inch cubes

2 tablespoons craisins (dried cranberries), chopped

1 teaspoon honey

1/8 teaspoon ground cumin

1/4 teaspoon white pepper

1/4 teaspoon cinnamon

Melt butter in a large nonstick skillet over medium to high heat. Add onion and chili pepper and fry about 2 minutes. Lower the heat to medium to low and add jicama and remaining ingredients. Continue cooking about 2 minutes, stirring frequently. Remove from the heat and let cool. Pour mixture into a medium bowl; use immediately, or cover and refrigerate up to 24 hours.

**32 servings
(1 tablespoon each)**
Calories: 19
Protein: 0
Carbohydrates: 2 gm
Fat: 1 gm

Peach and Onion Salsa

A snappy salsa for grilled or broiled chicken or turkey, or for dipping with tortilla chips.

Makes about 4 1/2 cups

2 pounds ripe peaches, peeled and cut into chunks

2 tablespoons fresh lemon juice

1 1/2 cups chopped red bell pepper

1 1/4 cups chopped sweet onions

2 tablespoons curry powder

1/2 teaspoon cayenne pepper

1/2 cup firmly packed golden brown sugar

1/2 cup cider vinegar

1/2 cup coarsely chopped fresh cilantro

Combine peaches and lemon juice in medium bowl. Place bell pepper and onion in medium nonstick saucepan. Stir over medium to low heat until vegetables are crisp to tender, about 6 minutes. Add curry powder and cayenne pepper to saucepan and stir 1 minute. Add brown sugar and stir until dissolved, about 2 minutes. Add cider vinegar; stir 2 minutes. Add peach mixture and accumulated juices to saucepan and cook until heated through, about 3 minutes.

Pour into medium bowl and cool completely. Add cilantro and mix well. Serve right away, or cover and refrigerate. Use within a week.

**72 servings
(1 tablespoon each)**
Calories: 12
Protein: 0
Carbohydrates: 3 gm
Fat: 0

Zucchini and Pineapple Salsa

Use this wonderful salsa as a topping for salads or on boiled or fried rice. It also makes a good dip with tortilla chips.

Makes about 4 1/2 cups

2 cups diced, unpeeled zucchini

15 1/4-ounce can crushed pineapple, drained

1/4 cup craisins (dried cranberries), diced

1/4 cup diced red onion

3 tablespoons lime juice

1 jalapeño chili pepper, seeded and diced

1 tablespoon chopped fresh cilantro

2 teaspoons olive oil

Combine all the ingredients in a large bowl. Mix well. Serve soon or cover and refrigerate up to 3 days.

**72 servings
(1 tablespoon each)**
Calories: 7
Protein: 0
Carbohydrates: 2 gm
Fat: 0

Cucumber Mango Salsa

 This is a great addition to fruit soup and some vegetable soups; it's also lovely in black bean soup.

Makes about 2 1/2 cups

1 small cucumber, cut into 1/4-inch cubes

3 tablespoons chopped red onion

3 tablespoons lime juice

1 medium ripe mango cut into 1/2-inch cubes

1/4 teaspoon crushed, dried hot red chilies

1/2 teaspoon grated fresh ginger

Combine all the ingredients in a medium bowl. Mix well. Serve right away or cover and refrigerate. Use within a day.

**40 servings
(1 tablespoon each)**
Calories: 5
Protein: 0
Carbohydrates: 1 gm
Fat: 0

Cucumber Lime Salsa

**Serve over grilled or broiled meats
or just serve with tortilla chips.**

Makes about 2 cups

1/2 cup lime juice

1/4 cup olive oil

3 tablespoons honey

1 fresno chili pepper, seeded and
    finely chopped

1/2 cup chopped green onions

2 cucumbers, peeled and diced small

1/4 cup chopped fresh cilantro

1/4 cup unsalted peanuts, finely
    chopped

Combine all the ingredients in
a medium bowl. Mix well.
Cover and refrigerate at least
1 hour before serving.

**32 servings
(1 tablespoon each)**

Calories: 32

Protein: 0

Carbohydrates: 3 gm

Fat: 2 gm

Spicy Cheese Pumpkin Salsa

This is a very tasty salsa for a dip, using your favorite variety of vegetable strips or tortilla chips, or spoon over mashed potatoes or rice.

Makes about 4 cups

3 cups shredded sharp cheddar cheese

8-ounce package cream cheese, softened

1 cup sour cream

3/4 cup canned pumpkin

3 green onions, finely chopped

1/2 cup finely chopped sweet red bell pepper

1/2 cup finely chopped fresh parsley leaves

1/2 teaspoon grated fresh ginger

1 serrano chili pepper, seeded and minced

1 teaspoon Dry Jerk Seasoning (see recipe page 3)

1 tablespoon extra virgin olive oil

1 tablespoon butter or margarine

In a large bowl, combine all the ingredients except the butter. Mix well. Melt butter in a large nonstick saucepan over medium heat. Pour cheese mixture into saucepan. Simmer, stirring frequently, until cheeses melt, about 5 minutes. Remove from the heat and pour mixture into a medium bowl; serve hot or at room temperature.

**64 servings
(1 tablespoon each)**

Calories: 47

Protein: 2 gm

Carbohydrates: 1 gm

Fat: 4 gm

Port Mushroom Salsa

A lovely topping over chicken, turkey, or pork chops.

Makes about 2 1/2 cups

2 tablespoons butter

1 3/4 cups sliced mushrooms

1 teaspoon minced garlic

1/2 cup tawny port

1/2 cup chicken stock or canned low-salt broth

1/2 cup whipping cream

3/4 teaspoon dried rosemary

Melt butter in a medium non-stick skillet over medium to high heat. Add mushrooms; sauté until golden, about 5 minutes. Transfer to plate. Add garlic to skillet and sauté 1 minute. Add port and bring to boil, scraping up any browned bits. Add stock, cream, and rosemary and boil until slightly thickened, about 5 minutes. Return mushrooms to skillet; stir until heated through, about 1 minute. Pour mixture into a medium bowl.

**40 servings
(1 tablespoon each)**
Calories: 14
Protein: 0
Carbohydrates: 0
Fat: 1 gm

Jalapeño and Peanut Salsa

Serve with grilled or broiled turkey steaks,
or spoon over leafy greens as a salad.

Makes about 2 1/2 cups

1 jalapeño chili pepper, seeded and
chopped

3/4 cup sweet and sour sauce

1/4 cup water

1 cup unsalted dry roasted peanuts,
finely chopped

2 tablespoons chopped parsley leaves

1/2 teaspoon minced garlic

1 tablespoon lime juice

Combine all the ingredients in
a 1-quart nonstick saucepan.
Bring to boil over medium
heat, stirring constantly. Cook
for 5 minutes, stirring occasionally. Remove the pan from
heat, and pour the salsa into a
medium bowl. Serve at room
temperature, or cover, refrigerate, and use within a week.

**40 servings
(1 tablespoon each)**
Calories: 27
Protein: 1 gm
Carbohydrates: 2 gm
Fat: 2 gm

Peanut Salsa

Serve as a dipping salsa for grilled or broiled chicken or pork or turkey strips. Good with fresh vegetable strips, too.

Makes about 1 cup

1/2 cup peanut butter

2 tablespoons chopped jalapeño chili pepper

1 teaspoon chopped sweet onion

1/4 cup lemon juice

1 teaspoon ground cinnamon

1/2 teaspoon ground cumin

1 tablespoon soy sauce

1/4 teaspoon chopped garlic

1/2 teaspoon ground coriander

Combine all the ingredients in a blender or food processor; process until smooth. Pour mixture into a medium bowl. This salsa can be covered and refrigerated up to 4 days before use but should be allowed to warm to room temperature before serving.

**16 servings
(1 tablespoon each)**
Calories: 50
Protein: 2 gm
Carbohydrates: 2 gm
Fat: 4 gm

Garlic Almond Salsa

For an incredible taste, serve this salsa on grilled or broiled meat or fish.

Makes about 2 1/2 cups

1 large russet potato, peeled and sliced

3/4 cup slivered almonds

3 tablespoons fresh lemon juice

3 large cloves garlic

1/4 teaspoon pepper

3/4 cup chicken stock or canned low-salt broth

1/4 cup olive oil

Cook potato slices in saucepan of boiling water until tender, about 15 minutes. Drain; transfer potato slices to food processor. Add almonds, lemon juice, garlic, and pepper; puree. With machine running, gradually add the stock, then the oil, in a very thin stream. Transfer sauce to bowl. Cover the bowl and cool (sauce will thicken). Let stand at room temperature. Serve.

**40 servings
(1 tablespoon each)**
Calories: 31
Protein: 1 gm
Carbohydrates: 1 gm
Fat: 3 gm

Unusual Salsas

Apple Lime Salsa

Serve with baked halibut, roasted leg of lamb, or barbecued pork loin.

Makes about 2 1/2 cups

1 medium red onion, finely chopped

2 fresno chili peppers, seeded and minced

2 Golden Delicious apples, cored and diced

3 tablespoons lime juice

1/2 teaspoon grated fresh ginger

1/8 teaspoon cumin

1/8 teaspoon cayenne pepper

Combine all the ingredients in a medium bowl. Mix well. Cover and refrigerate at least 1 hour before serving.

**40 servings
(1 tablespoon each)**
Calories: 6
Protein: 0
Carbohydrates: 2 gm
Fat: 0

Avocado and Sunflower Seed Salsa

Serve with any kind of firm white broiled fish or
as a tasty topping on a lettuce salad.

Makes about 2 cups

2 ripe avocados, peeled and chopped

1/2 cup chopped cilantro leaves

1 serrano chili pepper, seeded and
minced

1 1/3 cups fresh parsley leaves,
coarsely chopped

5 tablespoons shelled, roasted,
unsalted sunflower seeds

1 tablespoon lemon juice

1 tablespoon olive oil

Pinch of cayenne pepper

Combine all the ingredients
in a medium bowl. Gently stir
with a fork to mix without
mashing the avocado. Serve
right away.

**32 servings
(1 tablespoon each)**
Calories: 33
Protein: 1 gm
Carbohydrates: 1 gm
Fat: 3 gm

Banana Curry Salsa

Serve over steamed fish fillets or turkey, or serve on rice.

Makes about 1 cup

1/2 teaspoon olive oil

1/4 cup chopped sweet onion

2 ripe bananas (not overripe), quartered

1 shallot, quartered

1 clove garlic, halved

1 3/4 teaspoons curry powder

3/4 cup low-salt chicken broth

1 tablespoon rice vinegar

1 1/2 teaspoons honey

1 red jalapeño chili pepper

2 teaspoons finely shredded lime peel

In a medium nonstick skillet, heat oil over medium to high heat. Add onion, bananas, shallot, and garlic; sauté until tender, about 2 minutes. Add curry powder and sauté for 30 seconds. Add chicken broth and simmer for 5 minutes, stirring occasionally. Pour onion mixture and remaining ingredients into a food processor or blender. Process until smooth.

**16 servings
(1 tablespoon each)**
Calories: 20
Protein: 0
Carbohydrates: 5 gm
Fat: 0

Black-Eyed Pea and Bacon Salsa

 Use this great salsa as a dip with your favorite tortilla chips.

Makes about 5 1/2 cups

15-ounce can black-eyed peas, rinsed and drained

15-ounce can black beans, rinsed and drained

2 large tomatoes, seeded and chopped

1/3 cup finely diced radishes

1/2 cup finely diced onion

1 serrano chili pepper, seeded and finely diced

4 slices bacon, cooked, drained, and crumbled

2 tablespoons lime juice

2 tablespoons chopped fresh parsley

1 clove garlic, minced

1/8 teaspoon cayenne pepper

Combine all the ingredients in a large bowl. Mix well. Serve at room temperature.

**88 servings
(1 tablespoon each)**

Calories: 13

Protein: 1 gm

Carbohydrates: 2 gm

Fat: 0

Corn, Jicama, & Black Bean Salsa

 Serve rolled up in flour tortillas or over broiled or grilled chicken or pork dishes.

Makes about 4 cups

2 cups canned whole kernel corn, drained

1 cup diced jicama

1/2 cup canned black beans, rinsed and drained

1 cup minced red onion

1 serrano chili pepper, preferably red, seeded and diced

2 cloves garlic, minced

1/2 cup extra virgin olive oil

Place corn in a shallow baking pan. Broil corn 5 inches from heat (with electric oven door partially open) 5 to 10 minutes or until charred, stirring occasionally. Cool. Combine all ingredients in a medium bowl. Mix well. Cover and refrigerate overnight to allow flavors to blend before serving.

**64 servings
(1 tablespoon each)**
Calories: 23
Protein: 0
Carbohydrates: 2 gm
Fat: 2 gm

Craisin Ancho Chili Salsa

This salsa is a great topping over fried turkey or chicken or broiled pork chops.

Makes about 4 1/2 cups

1 cup craisins (dried cranberries)

3 tablespoons tequila

2 tablespoons olive oil

1 small onion, minced

3 cloves garlic, minced

1/2 cup dry sherry

1 dried ancho chili pepper, chopped

2 teaspoons minced fresh parsley

1 teaspoon pepper

1 teaspoon minced fresh thyme leaves

1/2 teaspoon minced fresh rosemary leaves

4 cups chicken broth

1 tablespoon cornstarch

1 tablespoon water

Small pinch cayenne pepper

Mince 1/2 cup of the craisins; set aside. In a small jar with lid, combine the tequila and remaining craisins; shake jar and let craisins moisten at least 1 hour or up to 2 days. Heat oil in large nonstick saucepan over high heat. When hot, add onion and garlic. Cook, stirring, until golden brown, about 5 minutes.

Add reserved minced craisins, sherry, chili pepper, parsley, pepper, thyme, and rosemary; stir until liquid evaporates. Add chicken broth; simmer over medium heat until reduced to 3 cups, about 20 minutes. Mix cornstarch with

1 tablespoon water. Slowly
whisk mixture into craisin
sauce and bring sauce to a
boil; boil 1 minute. Strain
sauce through a fine wire
strainer. Add cayenne and
tequila-soaked craisins to
sauce. Mix well. Keep sauce
warm in a double boiler. Or if
making ahead, cool, cover,
and chill for up to 2 days.
Reheat before serving.

**72 servings
(1 tablespoon each)**
Calories: 17
Protein: 0
Carbohydrates: 2 gm
Fat: 0

Craisin Orange Salsa

 This is a lovely topping on grilled or broiled lamb chops.

Makes about 1 1/2 cups

1 seedless orange, peeled and chopped

1/4 cup finely chopped sweet onion

1/4 cup jalapeño chili pepper

1/4 cup craisins (dried cranberries)

1 tablespoon grated orange zest

1 tablespoon minced parsley

1 tablespoon apple cider vinegar

Combine all the ingredients in a medium bowl. Mix well. Cover and refrigerate about 4 hours or overnight.

**24 servings
(1 tablespoon each)**

Calories: 9

Protein: 0

Carbohydrates: 2 gm

Fat: 0

Green Onion Salsa

A delicious salsa for grilled or broiled meat or fish.

Makes about 3 1/2 cups

1 tablespoon olive oil

2 bunches green onions, sliced (about 2 1/2 cups)

1 large shallot, coarsely chopped

1 large clove garlic, chopped

1 cup chopped fresh cilantro

1 whole green chili from can

1 cup chicken stock or canned unsalted broth

4 teaspoons fresh lime juice

Heat oil in a medium nonstick skillet over medium to low heat. Add onion, shallot, and garlic and cook just until crisp to tender, about 4 minutes. Combine chopped cilantro and chili in food processor or blender. Add onion mixture and chicken stock and puree until smooth. Return sauce to same skillet. Heat sauce over low heat. Stir in lime juice. Serve.

**56 servings
(1 tablespoon each)**
Calories: 6
Protein: 0
Carbohydrates: 1 gm
Fat: 0

Jalapeño Tartar Salsa

 A lovely topping for crab cakes and fish fillets or steaks.

Makes about 1 1/2 cups

1 cup nonfat mayonnaise

1 jalapeño chili pepper, seeded and minced

1 small sour pickle, finely chopped

2 tablespoons finely chopped purple onion

1 tablespoon finely chopped parsley

1 teaspoon finely chopped tarragon

1 tablespoon lemon juice

1 teaspoon Dijon mustard

Combine all ingredients in a medium bowl; mix well. Cover and refrigerate it until serving time.

**24 servings
(1 tablespoon each)**

Calories: 8

Protein: 0

Carbohydrates: 2 gm

Fat: 0

Mango Salsa

 This salsa can accompany almost any grilled or broiled fish, especially a meaty steak like swordfish or tuna.

Makes about 2 1/2 cups

1 large ripe mango, diced

1 tablespoon honey

1/4 cup sliced scallions, including some green tops

1/2 cup diced red bell pepper

1 tablespoon lime juice

1 teaspoon grated lime rind

1 1/2 teaspoons minced garlic

1/2 teaspoon fresh grated ginger

1 jalapeño chili pepper, seeded and minced

1/4 teaspoon ground mace

1 tablespoon chopped fresh parsley

Combine all the ingredients in a medium bowl. Mix well. Cover the bowl, and refrigerate for at least 1 hour before serving.

**40 servings
(1 tablespoon each)**
Calories: 6
Protein: 0
Carbohydrates: 2 gm
Fat: 0

Nopalito Salsa

Use this tasty salsa as you would any other: with meats, chips, and over leafy greens as a salad.

Makes about 3 1/2 cups

1 1/3 cups canned or bottled nopalitos, rinsed, drained, and diced

11-ounce jar or 1 1/3 cups diced
cooked green beans

3/4 cup diced jicama

2 small tomatoes, diced

1/2 cup diced onion

1/4 cup chopped fresh cilantro

3 tablespoons red wine vinegar

1 tablespoon olive oil

1 serrano chili pepper, minced

1 clove garlic, minced

Combine all ingredients in a medium bowl; mix well. Cover and refrigerate until well chilled, about 2 hours. Use within 1 week.

**56 servings
(1 tablespoon each)**
Calories: 7
Protein: 0
Carbohydrates: 1 gm
Fat: 0

Asian-Style Onion Salsa

 This salsa is excellent on tuna burgers or grilled steak.

Makes 1 cup

1 tablespoon sesame seeds

1 tablespoon lime juice

1/2 teaspoon oriental sesame oil

1 tablespoon low-sodium soy sauce

1/2 teaspoon sake (rice wine)

1 teaspoon honey

1/8 teaspoon dried crushed red pepper

1 cup finely chopped sweet onion

1/4 cup thinly sliced green onions

2 tablespoons finely chopped sweet red bell pepper

Place sesame seeds in a small, heavy nonstick skillet. Stir over medium to low heat until seeds are light golden, about 2 minutes. Cool. In a medium bowl, stir lime juice, sesame oil, soy sauce, sake, honey, and crushed red pepper; toss to blend. Add sesame seeds and remaining ingredients. Mix well. Serve.

**16 servings
(1 tablespoon each)**
Calories: 11
Protein: 0
Carbohydrates: 2 gm
Fat: 0

Onion Radish Salsa

Serve with grilled or broiled chicken, fish fillet, or pork chops.

Makes about 2 cups

1 1/2 cups chopped sweet onions

1 cup chopped radishes

2 tablespoons olive oil

2 tablespoons apple cider vinegar

1 1/2 teaspoons chopped fresh
    oregano

1/2 teaspoon ground cumin

Soak chopped onions in ice water about 1 hour; drain and transfer to medium bowl. Stir in remaining ingredients. Cover and refrigerate up to 3 hours.

**32 servings
(1 tablespoon each)**
Calories: 10
Protein: 0
Carbohydrates: 1 gm
Fat: 1 gm

Papaya Salsa

This is pleasant as a topping on grilled chicken, as a side dish with grilled or whole baked fish, or served with a skewer of shrimp.

Makes about 3 cups

1 tablespoon olive oil

1 red onion, minced

1 jalapeño chili pepper, seeded and minced

1/2 cup chopped red bell pepper

3 cloves garlic, minced

2 cups seeded and diced ripe papaya

1/2 tomato, seeded and chopped

2 tablespoons chopped fresh cilantro

1 teaspoon chopped fresh parsley

Heat oil in a medium nonstick skillet over medium heat. Add onion and cook until transparent, about 4 minutes. Add the peppers and cook about 5 minutes more. Add the remaining ingredients. Reduce heat and simmer, uncovered, for about 5 minutes. Remove from heat and let cool. Serve.

**48 servings
(1 tablespoon each)**
Calories: 6
Protein: 0
Carbohydrates: 1 gm
Fat: 0

Peanut Garlic Salsa

Serve over grilled or broiled meat or fish, poached fish, or mashed potatoes.

Makes about 2 cups

8 cloves garlic, minced

2 fresno chili peppers, seeded and chopped

1 1/2 cups unsalted peanuts, finely chopped

1/2 cup cilantro leaves, coarsely chopped

1/2 cup lime juice

1/4 cup olive oil

Combine all the ingredients in a medium bowl. Mix well. Serve soon, or cover, refrigerate, and use within a week.

**32 servings
(1 tablespoon each)**
Calories: 57
Protein: 2 gm
Carbohydrates: 2 gm
Fat: 5 gm

Pineapple and Red Pepper Salsa

This colorful salsa is a grand, not at all hot, accompaniment to a grilled or broiled fish steak such as tuna, swordfish, or salmon.

Makes about 1 1/2 cups

1/2 cup dry white wine

1/4 cup apple cider vinegar

1 cup finely chopped fresh pineapple

1/4 cup finely chopped red onion

1/4 cup finely diced red bell pepper

1 jalapeño chili pepper, seeded and minced

2 tablespoons finely chopped fresh parsley

Combine the wine and vinegar in a small nonstick saucepan and bring to a boil. Reduce the heat and simmer until the liquid has been reduced to about 1/4 cup. Stir in the pineapple, onion, red bell pepper, and jalapeño. Cook over low heat for 5 minutes. Remove the pan from the heat and pour the salsa into a small bowl. When it has cooled, cover and refrigerate it. Before serving the salsa, stir in the parsley.

24 servings
(1 tablespoon each)

Calories: 8

Protein: 0

Carbohydrates: 1 gm

Fat: 0

Red Pepper Salsa

 This salsa makes a great snack or hors d'oeuvre for a dinner party teamed with pita bread triangles and a variety of raw vegetables.

Makes about 2 cups

2 large cloves garlic, chopped

15-ounce can garbanzo beans (chick-peas), drained

1/3 cup tahini (sesame seed paste)

1/3 cup fresh lemon juice

1/2 cup chopped, drained, roasted red pepper from jar

With food processor running, drop garlic through feed tube and mince. Scrape down sides of bowl. Add chick-peas, tahini, and lemon juice; process until mixture is smooth. Add roasted peppers; process until peppers are finely chopped. Transfer sauce to small bowl. Serve at room temperature.

Note: Tahini is available at natural foods stores and some supermarkets.

**32 servings
(1 tablespoon each)**
Calories: 38
Protein: 2 gm
Carbohydrates: 4 gm
Fat: 2 gm

Ginger, Papaya, & Red Pepper Salsa

Serve over grilled or broiled plump white-fleshed fish.

Makes about 2 cups

1 teaspoon olive oil

1 clove garlic, finely chopped

1 tablespoon finely chopped fresh ginger

1/2 teaspoon red pepper flakes

1/2 cup white wine vinegar

3 tablespoons honey

2 ripe papayas, seeded and diced

1 red bell pepper, roasted, seeded, and diced

2 tablespoons lime juice

1/4 teaspoon ground black pepper

1/8 teaspoon sesame oil

In a nonstick skillet, heat olive oil over medium heat. Add garlic, ginger, and red pepper flakes and sauté until the garlic begins to turn brown, about 1 minute. Add vinegar, honey, and half of the papaya; cook until the papaya starts to fall apart and the sauce thickens, 6 to 8 minutes. Add the remaining papaya and roasted red pepper and cook until the salsa is just warmed through. (Do not overcook: you want to preserve the diced raw papaya texture.) Season with lime juice, black pepper, and sesame oil. Remove from heat. Pour mixture into a medium bowl. Cover and let sit 10 minutes to allow flavors to blend before serving.

**32 servings
(1 tablespoon each)**
Calories: 17
Protein: 0
Carbohydrates: 4 gm
Fat: 0

Pumpkin Seed Salsa

 This salsa makes a great dip for your favorite tortilla chips.

Makes about 1 1/2 cups

1/4 cup unsalted pumpkin seeds

2 tablespoons chopped onion

1 tablespoon chopped jalapeño chili pepper

1 tablespoon water

2 sprigs fresh cilantro

1/4 teaspoon sugar

1/8 teaspoon black pepper

1 clove garlic, peeled

In a small nonstick skillet, cook pumpkin seeds over medium heat 5 minutes or until lightly browned, stirring constantly. Remove from the heat. Pour seeds into a food processor; process until finely ground. Add the remaining ingredients and process until smooth. Pour mixture into a small nonstick saucepan and place over low heat; cook 3 minutes or until thoroughly heated, stirring frequently. Serve.

**24 servings
(1 tablespoon each)**

Calories: 9

Protein: 0

Carbohydrates: 0

Fat: 1 gm

Rhubarb Strawberry Salsa

Serve it with chicken, turkey, or your favorite variety of fruits, or spoon over leafy greens as a salad.

Makes about 4 1/2 cups

1 cup sugar

1/4 cup water

1 tablespoon finely shredded orange peel

6 cups rhubarb, sliced 1/2-inch thick

1 cup frozen unsweetened strawberries, thawed

2 tablespoons honey

1 serrano chili pepper, seeded and cut into chunks

2 tablespoons lemon juice

1/4 teaspoon ground mace

In a medium nonstick saucepan, combine sugar, water, and orange peel. Bring to a boil over high heat. Add rhubarb; reduce heat. Simmer gently until the rhubarb is very tender, about 20 minutes. Remove mixture from heat. Let rhubarb cool to room temperature. Pour mixture in food processor and process until smooth. Scrape the puree into a large bowl. Puree the remaining ingredients in food processor until smooth. Stir the strawberry puree into the rhubarb puree. Mix well. Serve at room temperature or chilled.

**72 servings
(1 tablespoon each)**
Calories: 16
Protein: 0
Carbohydrates: 4 gm
Fat: 0

Spicy Succotash Salsa

 This is a great filling for pita pockets or rolled up in flour tortillas, or on shredded lettuce as a salad. It's perfect all by itself, too.

Makes about 3 cups

1 pound thawed frozen yellow corn

2 10-ounce packages thawed frozen lima beans

1/4 cup dry white wine

1 cup hulled, roasted, unsalted sunflower seeds

1 clove garlic, minced

2 jalapeño chili peppers, seeded and diced

1 tablespoon olive oil

1 tablespoon chopped cilantro

1/2 cup diced sweet red pepper

1/8 teaspoon cayenne pepper

In large nonstick skillet over medium to high heat, combine corn, lima beans and wine. Cover and cook until hot and most liquid has evaporated, about 10 minutes. Stir in remaining ingredients. Remove from heat. Serve warm.

**48 servings
(1 tablespoon each)**
Calories: 41
Protein: 2 gm
Carbohydrates: 5 gm
Fat: 2 gm

Tomato and Mango Salsa

 Serve over chicken or turkey or spoon onto tortilla chips.

Makes about 2 cups

1 tomato, finely chopped

3/4 cup finely chopped mango

3 tablespoons finely chopped purple onion

2 tablespoons finely chopped fresh basil

2 tablespoons red wine vinegar

Combine all the ingredients in a medium bowl. Mix well. Cover and refrigerate at least 30 minutes.

32 servings (1 tablespoon each)

Calories: 4

Protein: 0

Carbohydrates: 1 gm

Fat: 0

Tomato, Sunflower Seed, & Scallion Salsa

 This salsa is perfect with egg dishes, over angel hair pasta, or served with fried rice.

Makes about 3 1/2 cups

1 cup shelled, roasted, unsalted sunflower seeds

4 serrano chili peppers, coarsely chopped

Tops from 2 bunches of scallions, coarsely chopped

1 large ripe tomato or 2 plum tomatoes, diced

1/4 cup finely shredded fresh basil leaves

2 teaspoons lemon juice

1/2 cup olive oil

1 cup water

1/8 teaspoon grated fresh ginger

Combine all the ingredients in a medium bowl. Mix well. Serve soon, or cover, refrigerate, and use within a day.

**56 servings
(1 tablespoon each)**
Calories: 34
Protein: 1 gm
Carbohydrates: 1 gm
Fat: 3 gm

Chunky Tuna Salsa

A wonderful tasting salsa; serve with tortilla chips or on your favorite cracker.

Makes about 2 1/2 cups

6 1/2-ounce can tuna, well drained

1 red onion, chopped

1/2 cup finely chopped jicama

1 large tomato, chopped

1 jalapeño chili pepper, seeded and minced

1 clove garlic, minced

1 tablespoon lemon juice

1/8 teaspoon black pepper

Break up tuna with fork. Combine tuna and the remaining ingredients in a medium bowl. Gently stir with fork to mix. Cover the bowl and refrigerate at least 1 hour before serving.

**40 servings
(1 tablespoon each)**
Calories: 8
Protein: 1 gm
Carbohydrates: 1 gm
Fat: 0

Shrimp Salsa

**Serve with your favorite tortilla chips
or over leafy greens as a salad.**

Makes about 6 1/2 cups

2 6-ounce packages large cooked
  cocktail shrimp

6 tablespoons lime juice

1/2 teaspoon ground turmeric

1 teaspoon sugar

1 cup diced yellow pepper (1/4-inch
  pieces)

1 cup diced red pepper (1/4-inch
  pieces)

1 1/2 teaspoons minced garlic

1/4 cup finely chopped green onion,
  green and white part

3 jalapeño chili peppers, finely
  chopped

1/2 cup finely chopped jicama

1 avocado, diced in 1/4-inch pieces

2 teaspoons olive oil

Thaw and drain shrimp, then
coarsely chop. In a small
bowl, stir lime juice, turmeric,
and sugar; mix until dis-
solved. In a large bowl, mix
shrimp and 8 remaining
ingredients. Add lime juice
mixture and mix well. Serve.

104 servings
(1 tablespoon each)
Calories: 8
Protein: 1 gm
Carbohydrates: 1 gm
Fat: 0

Salmon Salsa

Serve as a dip for tortilla chips and crackers
or for assorted bite-size vegetables.

Makes about 1 cup

6 ounces cooked skinless salmon

1/4 cup unflavored yogurt

2 tablespoons minced onion

2 tablespoons olive oil

1 tablespoon lemon juice

1 tablespoon Dijon mustard

3/4 teaspoon dry dill weed

1 teaspoon minced garlic

1/8 teaspoon ground cayenne pepper

Break up salmon with fork.
Combine salmon and the
remaining ingredients in a
small bowl. Mix well. Cover
the bowl and refrigerate for at
least 1 hour before serving.

**16 servings
(1 tablespoon each)**
Calories: 39
Protein: 3 gm
Carbohydrates: 1 gm
Fat: 3 gm

Cilantro Cocktail Salsa

This salsa has a fine taste for grilled or broiled shrimp and it's great for oysters and mussels.

Makes about 1 1/2 cups

1 cup catsup

3 tablespoons finely chopped fresh cilantro

1/4 cup finely diced, unpeeled zucchini

2 tablespoons prepared white horseradish

2 tablespoons fresh lime juice

Combine all ingredients in small bowl. Mix well. Cover the bowl and refrigerate for at least 4 hours before serving. Use within 1 week.

**24 servings
(1 tablespoon each)**
Calories: 12
Protein: 0
Carbohydrates: 3 gm
Fat: 0

Caribbean Salsa

Serve this salsa with grilled or broiled fish.

Makes about 2 1/2 cups

1 large ripe banana, chopped

1/2 cup diced fresh pineapple

1/2 cup finely chopped sweet red bell pepper

1/2 cup finely chopped sweet green bell pepper

1/2 cup chopped fresh cilantro

3 green onions, finely chopped

1 roasted jalapeño chili pepper, chopped

1 tablespoon minced ginger

2 tablespoons brown sugar

3 tablespoons lime juice

1 tablespoon olive oil

1/8 teaspoon pepper

Combine all the ingredients in a medium bowl. Mix gently and thoroughly. Cover the bowl and refrigerate for at least 2 hours before serving.

Note: To roast jalapeños, place on a foil-lined baking sheet. Broil 5 inches from heat 5 minutes on each side or until blistered. Place in a heavy duty plastic bag; let stand 10 minutes. Peel and seed pepper.

**40 servings
(1 tablespoon each)**
Calories: 10
Protein: 0
Carbohydrates: 2 gm
Fat: 0

Tropical Salsa

 Spoon over broiled or grilled fish or poultry.

Makes about 2 cups

1 teaspoon olive oil

1 clove garlic, finely chopped

1 ripe mango, finely chopped

2 green onions, white part only, finely chopped

Pinch cayenne pepper

1/2 cup sweet red pepper, seeded and diced

1 teaspoon grated fresh ginger

1/8 teaspoon black pepper

1/4 teaspoon ground nutmeg

1 tablespoon lemon juice

In a nonstick skillet, heat oil over medium heat. Add garlic and sauté until the garlic begins to turn brown, about 1 minute. Remove from heat. Pour garlic into a medium bowl and add the remaining ingredients, stirring to combine them well. Let sit 10 minutes to allow flavors to blend before serving.

**32 servings
(1 tablespoon each)**

Calories: 7

Protein: 0

Carbohydrates: 1 gm

Fat: 0

Herbed Turkey Salsa

For boiled or fried rice, this salsa is the topping.
Serve over hot pasta, like penne.

Makes about 4 1/2 cups

2 tablespoons olive oil

4 cloves garlic, chopped

1 pound ground turkey

14-ounce can crushed tomatoes with
   added puree

1/2 cup white wine vinegar

1/4 cup chopped fresh cilantro leaves

1/4 cup chopped fresh basil or
   3/4 tablespoon dried

2 teaspoons dried oregano leaves,
   finely crushed

1/2 teaspoon cumin

1/8 teaspoon cayenne pepper

2 jalapeño chili peppers, seeded and
   chopped

1/2 cup chopped green onions

2 tomatoes, finely chopped

In a large nonstick skillet, heat oil over medium heat. Add garlic and sauté until the garlic begins to turn brown, about 1 minute. Add turkey and sauté until it begins to brown, breaking up large chunks with spoon, about 8 minutes. Add next 7 ingredients, reduce heat to medium to low, and simmer mixture until thickened to sauce consistency, about 30 minutes. Add chili peppers, green onions, and tomatoes. Simmer until reduced to sauce consistency, about 5 minutes. Remove from heat. Serve.

**72 servings
(1 tablespoon each)**
Calories: 19
Protein: 1 gm
Carbohydrates: 1 gm
Fat: 1 gm

Sweet Salsas

Cranberry Ginger Salsa

This salsa is terrific as a topping for ice cream or fruit salad or as a syrup for pancakes or waffles.

Makes about 3 1/4 cups

12-ounce package cranberries

3/4 cup water

1 tablespoon sugar

1 1/2 teaspoons grated orange peel

1/2 teaspoon ground ginger

1/8 teaspoon ground mace

1/2 cup pure maple syrup

2 tablespoons finely chopped crystallized ginger

1/2 cup craisins (dried cranberries)

Combine cranberries, water, sugar, grated orange peel, ground ginger, and ground mace in medium nonstick saucepan over medium heat. Cook until cranberry skins burst, stirring frequently, about 5 minutes. Transfer sauce to food processor. Add maple syrup and process until almost smooth. Transfer sauce to medium bowl. Stir in chopped crystallized ginger and craisins. Cover the bowl and refrigerate overnight. Serve.

**52 servings
(1 tablespoon each)**

Calories: 17

Protein: 0

Carbohydrates: 4 gm

Fat: 0

Gingered Fruit Salsa

This salsa is a great topping for ice cream and cake, too. It gives a lift to bagels and pancakes.

Makes about 2 1/2 cups

1/2 cup raspberries

2 tablespoons sugar

3 tablespoons minced crystallized ginger

1/2 cup craisins (dried cranberries), chopped

1 ripe mango, finely diced

4 large strawberries, finely diced

1/2 cup finely diced fresh pineapple

1/2 teaspoon balsamic vinegar

In a medium bowl crush raspberries into large pieces with sugar and let stand 5 minutes. Stir in the remaining ingredients and mix well.

**40 servings
(1 tablespoon each)**

Calories: 16

Protein: 0

Carbohydrates: 4 gm

Fat: 0

Honey Ginger Salsa

This salsa is delicious with meat and fish.
The sweet taste is also nice for a dipping salsa.

Makes about 1 1/4 cups

8-ounce can sweetened tamarind
  nectar

1 tablespoon honey

1 1/2 tablespoons grated fresh ginger

1 tablespoon soy sauce

1 tablespoon Dry Jerk Seasoning
  (see recipe page 3)

1 teaspoon cornstarch

1 teaspoon water

Combine the tamarind nectar and honey in a medium non-stick saucepan over medium heat and boil until it has been reduced to about 3/4 cup. Stir in the ginger, soy sauce, and Dry Jerk Seasoning. Mix the cornstarch with the water to form a paste, and then mix with the tamarind mixture. Continue to cook, stirring frequently, until the sauce thickens. Serve hot or cold.

Note: Cans of tamarind nectar can be found in Oriental food stores.

**20 servings
(1 tablespoon each)**
Calories: 12
Protein: 0
Carbohydrates: 3 gm
Fat: 0

Honey Soy Salsa

 This makes a great glaze for chicken legs or pork loin.

Makes about 3/4 cup

3 tablespoons soy sauce

3 tablespoons honey

2 tablespoons red wine vinegar

1 teaspoon Dry Jerk Seasoning
  (see recipe page 3)

1 1/2 teaspoons cornstarch

1/4 cup water

Combine the soy sauce, honey, vinegar, and Dry Jerk Seasoning in a medium non-stick saucepan over medium heat and bring to a boil. Mix together the cornstarch and the water. Stir into the sauce and cook until thickened. Serve hot or cold.

**12 servings
(1 tablespoon each)**

Calories: 20

Protein: 0

Carbohydrates: 5 gm

Fat: 0

Kiwi Salsa

This is a minimally sweet salsa that goes well with grilled or broiled fish steaks such as salmon, swordfish, or tuna.

Makes about 1 cup

4 ripe kiwis, peeled and diced into 1/4-inch pieces

2 tablespoons finely chopped red onion

1/2 teaspoon grated orange rind

1 teaspoon grated fresh ginger

3 teaspoons orange juice

1 teaspoon olive oil

1/4 teaspoon freshly ground black pepper

1/8 teaspoon ground mace

Combine all the ingredients in a small bowl. Cover the bowl and refrigerate it until shortly before serving time. Serve the salsa at room temperature.

**16 servings
(1 tablespoon each)**
Calories: 15
Protein: 0
Carbohydrates: 3 gm
Fat: 0

Strawberry Salsa

 This lovely salsa can be served with your favorite variety of fruits and spooned over pancakes, French toast, or waffles.

Makes about 1 1/2 cups

1 cup frozen unsweetened whole strawberries, thawed

2 tablespoons honey

1 teaspoon grated orange rind

1 serrano chili pepper, seeded and cut into chunks

1 tablespoon lemon juice

1/8 teaspoon ground mace

Combine all the ingredients in a blender or food processor; process until smooth. Pour mixture into a medium bowl. Serve chilled or at room temperature.

**24 servings
(1 tablespoon each)**
Calories: 8
Protein: 0
Carbohydrates: 2 gm
Fat: 0

Tamarind Apricot Salsa

This can be served as a condiment with meat, fish, chicken, or vegetables.

Makes about 1 1/2 cups

8-ounce can sweetened tamarind nectar

4 ounces apricot jam

2 tablespoons honey

1 teaspoon Dijon mustard

Combine the tamarind nectar and apricot jam in a medium nonstick saucepan over medium heat and bring to a boil until the mixture thickens. Stir in the honey and mustard. Serve cold.

**24 servings
(1 tablespoon each)**

Calories: 24

Protein: 0

Carbohydrates: 6 gm

Fat: 0

Watermelon Dessert Salsa

 It looks like a diced fruit salad, but has a spicy kick. Spoon it over frozen low-fat yogurt or fruit sorbet and serve with biscotti cookies.

Makes about 3 cups

2 cups finely diced watermelon

1 ripe banana, diced

1 cup strawberries, coarsely chopped

2 tablespoons lemon juice

1 tablespoon honey

1/4 teaspoon ground mace

1/8 teaspoon cayenne pepper

Combine all the ingredients in a medium bowl. Cover and refrigerate at least 1 hour before serving.

48 servings (1 tablespoon each)

Calories: 7

Protein: 0

Carbohydrates: 2 gm

Fat: 0

Index